Postwar Civility

Westphalia Press Civility Series
westphaliapress.org

Volume 1
Revolutionary Civility
Rules of Decent Behavior in Company and Conversation

Volume 2
Expansive Civility
The American Chesterfield

Volume 3
Manifest Civility
The Young Man's Own Book

Volume 4
Industrial Civility
The Primer of Politeness

Volume 5
Progressive Civility
Wehman's Etiquette and Politeness

Volume 6
Civility and the Great War
The Stakes of Diplomacy

Volume 7
Postwar Civility
On Kindness

Postwar Civility

On Kindness

by Rev. J. Guibert

Volume 7 in the Westphalia Press Civility Series

WESTPHALIA PRESS
An imprint of Policy Studies Organization

On Kindness: Postwar Civility
All Rights Reserved © 2014 by Policy Studies Organization

Westphalia Press
An imprint of Policy Studies Organization
1527 New Hampshire Ave., NW
Washington, D.C. 20036
dgutierrezs@ipsonet.org

ISBN-13: 978-1935907626
ISBN-10: 193590762X

Cover design by Taillefer Long at Illuminated Stories:
www.illuminatedstories.com

Updated material and comments on this edition
can be found at the Westphalia Press website:
www.westphaliapress.org

In Search of Civility

An archaic meaning of civility was 'study of the humanities,' and as a word it appears in the sixteenth century. The years have not blunted its importance; it is one of the guiding principles of *Wikipedia*, which informs readers that, "The civility policy is a standard of conduct that sets out how *Wikipedia* editors should interact. Stated simply, editors should always treat each other with consideration and respect. In order to keep the focus on improving the encyclopedia and to help maintain a pleasant editing environment, editors should behave politely, calmly and reasonably, even during heated debates."

Other voices also have been raised about the need to consider civility as a priority in an increasingly abrasive modern society. The Institute for Civility in Government in Houston, ably led by Cassandra Dahnke and Tomas Spath, has for many years hosted Washington seminars and blogs on the subject. Professor J.M. Forni at Johns Hopkins has made a life's work out of studying the ramifications of civility. In the Hopkins alumni magazine he sums the current situation up when he writes:

We do have our manners. What we have lost are the manners of past generations. That we have manners, however, does not mean we ought to be perfectly happy with the manners we have. In fact, many Americans think that civility and manners are in decline, that this decline has increased in the past several years, and that there is a causal connection between incivility and violence. Does reality match the perception of a decline? Yes and no. There is little doubt that we are losing established forms of deference and respect. On the other hand, new forms of respect take the place of those becoming obsolete. A pregnant woman may not easily find a youngster willing to give her his seat on a bus. But the number of men willing to treat the same woman as an intellectual peer on the job is higher today than it was yesterday.

This does not mean that we should ignore the coarsening of social interaction that we have been witnessing in recent years. Our manners inevitably suffer when:
1. We are poorly trained in self-restraint.
2. We are used to seeing others as means to the satisfaction of our desires rather than ends in themselves.
3. We are overly concerned about financial gain and professional achievement.
4. We are constantly besieged by stress and fatigue.
5. We are surrounded by strangers who will remain strangers.
When some or all of these factors are at work, it becomes difficult to be considerate — and consideration is the ethical requirement of manners that are really good.

Clearly we need more people to take an interest in the topic rather than less. The Westphalia Press Civility Series demonstrates that the topic has many aspects, including etiquette and diplomacy. My friend Ambassador Mark Hambley suggests that there even might be some connection between the decline of cursive writing and the decline of civility. Unfortunately the current lack of civility in Washington is as noticeable or more noticeable than the state of the nation's handwriting. While politics has always been a competitive sport, common consensus is that the political life in the capital recently has become far more contentious than in recent memory.

The Westphalia Press Civility Series presents manners, etiquette, diplomacy, decent behavior, and politeness as fruit in the same orchard. The books are intended to be an accessible resource for studying facets of a subject that we think contributes to the current policy anxiety that has paralyzed decision making.

The subject has a universal aspect. Although we relish including George Washington as author of one of the titles in the collection, he actually found many of the maxims in his *Rules of Civility* in the literature of French Jesuits of the 1590s that was rendered in English by Francis Hawkins in London in 1640. By all account he was a man of manners no matter what the circumstances, and so we respectfully dedicate this series to his memory, in hopes that present day leaders will reflect on his example.

Paul Rich
President, Policy Studies Organization
Garfield House, Washington, D.C.

H

ON KINDNESS

ON KINDNESS

By the

VERY REV. J. GUIBERT, S.S.
Superior of the Seminary of the
Catholic Institute, Paris

*Published by arrangement with
Burns, Oates and Washbourne, Ltd.
London*

ST. ANTHONY GUILD PRESS
PATERSON, NEW JERSEY

PREFACE

A MAN is never tired of hearing about what he cares much for; neither ought his fellow-men to weary of telling him things needful for him to know.

Now, there is nothing in our neighbour's dealings with us more engaging than kindness; yet of no duty do we require to be more frequently reminded than of that of being kind.

This thought has emboldened the author of the following pages to write in his turn on a subject treated before him by very many others.

Man's heart opens to kindness because it is to him a promise of coming happiness; he clings to it because he looks to it for the healing of the ills he suffers, which mostly are either pain or shame or neglect.

For each of these ills, kindness has a remedy.

Kindness dulls the edge of pain, for it is the true expression of pity, and ever inspires the bestowing of charitable help.

Kindness sweetens the bitterness of humiliation, for it is indulgent to faults, and openly respects the misunderstood and the persecuted.

In fine, by inspiring anew the Christian love of one's neighbour, kindness peoples the dreariest mental solitudes, and dispels the weary sadness of forsaken souls.

Nevertheless, just as much as men long for others to be kind to them, so are they themselves slow to grow in this virtue, and remiss in its practice.

Therefore is it so important to stir up in ourselves the instinctive kindliness which God has implanted in the depths of every human soul, but which too often is stifled out of life by selfishness.

Every single kind act we do makes us better; it marks one more victory gained by man over the evil instincts of his lower being; it is a fresh rising up of the human nature that fell in Adam, for it means the prevailing of its loftier impulses, and bears witness that it has been freed from the brutal yoke of the passions.

Of all things, then, a kindly spirit is most to be desired, since it not only perfects him who possesses it, but in the good deeds it inspires, tends to the happiness of all others.

Should the perusal of these pages inspire in the reader's heart a wish to cultivate the virtue of kindness, the author will have attained what he was working for.

CONTENTS

Page

PREFACE v

CHAPTER I

ON THE EXCEEDING WORTH OF KINDNESS

I. How kindness is a virtue of great price 1

II. How all men love the kind-hearted 8

III. How his own kind-heartedness makes the kind man happy 12

IV. How kindness overcomes all things 17

CHAPTER II

ON THE NATURE OF TRUE KINDNESS

I. How true kindness is compassionate 27

II. How true kindness is generous 38

III. How true kindness is gracious	52
IV. How true kindness is loving	65

CHAPTER III

On the Way to Become Kind

I. How the sort of mind a man has leads to his being kind-hearted or otherwise	77
II. How a man cannot be truly kind unless he has the will to be so	92
III. How true kindliness is a quality of the heart	104
IV. How it is religion that makes us kind	117

CHAPTER IV

On the Counterfeits of Kindness

I. Weakness of character	133
II. Flattery	142
III. Indiscreetness	148
IV. Emotional affection	152
Conclusion	158

ON KINDNESS

Chapter I

ON THE EXCEEDING WORTH OF KINDNESS

I

HOW KINDNESS IS A VIRTUE OF GREAT PRICE

KINDNESS is to be felt rather than to be defined. It is better to experience it than to try to explain what it is. Moreover, its home is in the heart rather than in the intellect.

When closely looked at, kindness seems a very complex virtue; or, peradventure with greater truth, we might say that kindness is not so much a single virtue as a happy admixture of many.

Sometimes it takes the form of a special affection, manifesting itself by gentleness, affability, obligingness, amiability and graciousness. Sometimes it takes a more active form, inspiring zeal, generosity, devotedness and self-denial. But oftener it is, externally, hardly more than passive, enabling the kind man to practise patience and endurance, to be indulgent and sympathetic with others, to forgive injuries, and humbly to forget himself.

That so many virtues need unite to build it up proves the worth of kindness. Its beauty and its fragrance are enhanced by its coming before us in the guise of a basket of many flowers.

If, nevertheless, it be insisted upon that we define what we mean by kindness, we are content that it be taken as that disposition of soul which inclines a man to wish well to others, and to seek to do them good. We mean,

THE WORTH OF KINDNESS

moreover, that it be deep-rooted in the innermost being of man, else it must needs be insincere. Kindness begins its work by making the kind man think well of others, and feel for others. This is that goodwill which suggests words of sympathy, and has its further expression in devotedness. Absolute unselfishness is its final development, for the thoroughly kind man hardly acts save for the sake of others. A man is kind in proportion as he is forgetful of his own earthly interests; and as he gives himself — sacrifices himself — for the good of others.

Kindness is a retiring virtue. It is not striking like genius, nor noisy like martial valour; in silence and in the dark it does good, and therewith is content. Kindness is not of the proud plants which flower only on the heights, it loves the fertile lowliness of hidden valleys; it is among those humble virtues which, in the charming thought of

St. Francis of Sales, blossom only at the foot of the Cross.

But, Father Faber says: "The grass of the field is better than the cedars of Lebanon. It feeds more, and it rests the eye better — that thymy daisy-eyed carpet, making earth sweet and fair and homelike. Kindness is the turf of the spiritual world, whereon the sheep of Christ feed quietly beneath the Shepherd's eye."*

That kindness is prone to conceal itself takes nothing from its worth; for if, as a rule, it excites no wondering admiration, it surely wins love. Alone, the kindness of an action reaches down to the innermost fibres of the human soul, and literally seizes the heart of man. And St. Paul puts it above all besides: "If I speak with the tongues of men and of angels; ... if I should have prophecy and should know all

---

*"Spiritual Conferences," chapter I, section 4.

mysteries, and all knowledge; and if I should have all faith so that I could remove mountains; ... and if I should deliver my body to be burned and have not charity" (of which, kindness is the expression), "I am become as sounding brass or a tinkling cymbal" (1 Cor. xiii. 1-4).

Of a truth, this lesson the fervent Apostle had learned in the school of his Master. For Jesus Christ, whom our faith bids us adore as God Incarnate, in coming to us has so veiled all the splendour of His Everlasting Majesty, that our eyes see naught in Him save His goodwill to man. He hides His glory, He puts not forward the deep knowledge of all things which is His, He commands not signs in the heavens, but wills only to be and to appear good to men. "Come unto Me," He has said, "and I will refresh you: him who cometh to Me I will in no way cast out." Nor, indeed, has He ever rejected anyone, He who opens

His arms to all mankind, to the insignificant, to the poor, to sinners, to all who by any are cast out. He who, by the splendour of His might, could have dazzled the eyes of all the children of men, has willed one thing only — to win their love.

Nor on His disciples did he enjoin aught that was striking in the eyes of men. They had but to love one another, to be merciful and meek: on this condition they were to make the conquest of the world. "Love one another," He said; "I send you as lambs among wolves." They will not be worthy of Him except they spare the broken reed, and stay their hands from quenching the smoking flax.

It was with a heart filled with Christ's goodwill to men that Lacordaire said: "It is God's goodwill to men which makes them love Him, and the man who lacks goodwill to others will never gain their love.... Goodness to others is that in which man most resembles God, and by which he most easily disarms his fellow-man.... Neither fame nor the affection of others gives the measure of the height reached by a soul, but its own kindliness, and its own kindliness only."

But why borrow from others phrases in praise of kindness? However rarely we may have experienced it at the hands of others, we each one of us realize its supreme worth and feel what it can achieve. We are drawn by it when, coming from the hearts of others, it envelops us in its warm and soothing atmosphere. Again, it makes us happy when it goes out from ourselves as the very purest expression of our souls. In fine, in our endeavour to call other men to a share in our thoughts and in our hopes, it is by the goodwill we show towards them that we shall win over their souls.

II

HOW ALL MEN LOVE THE KIND-HEARTED

Kindness shown to ourselves attracts and charms us. We are won on the instant by the happy confidence it inspires.

Even as a flower unfolds its petals to the rising sun, or as a bud opens under the soft breath of spring, so does the heart of man open to kindness.

The kindness we experience from others, like the life-giving air our lungs call out for, plunges, as it were, our whole being into an atmosphere of joy.

When we are sad the mere seeing of a kind face cheers us; when we are worried or anxious a kind and encouraging word is often all that is needed to ease our minds; when tortured by fear for our future, a self-sacrificing act of kindness on the part of some friend makes us realize that we have

THE WORTH OF KINDNESS

still something to lean upon, and confidence is born anew within us.

As Father Faber very truly remarks: "Kindness makes life bearable." For life, that most precious of gifts, passionately though we love it, weighs as a heavy burden on our shoulders, so great is the proportion of toil and of suffering in each one of our lots.

Under this "cross" (for verily a cross is all life upon earth) some fall to rise no more, others ever march bravely onwards. Why this difference? May it not be that some lose heart because they know not how to hope? Others, their hearts enlarged by happiness, are rushed on by the very joy of their being. Of a truth, facing life, man is strong or weak according as he is cheerful or sad at heart.

Sadness quenches the living fire within him, happiness is as fuel to it. And what breath better than that of a kindness received, to fan the flames of joy in a man's heart?

To impart, then, moral strength to thy fellow-man, be kind to him.

Hundreds of times each one of us has felt the happy effects of the kindness of others. Their kind looks have cheered us in hours of gloom: their kind words have fallen on our ears like music from heaven, and gently lulled our pain.

Nor, save when thus made happy, have we undertaken aught of great things for God or for our brethren.

Kindness has this power over us because it is the expression of the two sentiments that arouse us most effectually to action — esteem and sympathy; but for these our mind and will are starved.

For just as the humiliating disdain of the rich discourages the poor even more than it makes them suffer, so is it hard for any one of us to practise virtue when treated with contempt, or to open our hearts to what is good while shivering in an atmosphere of indifference.

To the man who feels that he is neither esteemed nor loved, the temptation to stop trying is perilously near. Kindnesses received keep us up precisely because they mean a liking for us, and are themselves a pledge of sympathy. The bearing of the man who acts from kindness is condescending, doubtless; but his is a condescension which honours others, which raises them in their own eyes, which betrays affection such as touches the heart and makes it beat the faster for very joy.

When a kindness has been done us our life is keener, for we have been stirred up, ennobled, heart-warmed. This is why we instinctively like kind people. They are to us a refuge, like the arms of a mother to her child.

III

HOW HIS OWN KIND-HEARTEDNESS MAKES THE KIND MAN HAPPY

To receive kindnesses from others is not, however, the greatest of all earthly happiness, for there is more joy in being kind oneself than in feeling that our fellow-men are kind to us. It is in the kind man's heart, wherefrom it unceasingly springs, that the stream of kindliness is at its fullest; there its very might enraptures; thence for it to overflow is beneficently to evaporate. "Happiness," writes Joubert, "means the feeling that one's own soul is full of goodwill; strictly speaking, there is no happiness other than this, against which sorrow itself is powerless." Father Faber has well described the happy effects which kind thoughts and words produce in the soul which inspires them: "The interior beauty of a soul through habitual kindliness of thought is greater than our words can tell. To such a man, life is a perpetual bright evening, with all things calm, and fragrant, and restful. The dust of life is laid, and its fever cool. All sounds are softer, as is the way of evening, and all sights are fairer, and the golden light makes our enjoyment of earth a happily pensive preparation for heaven."* "Kind words," he says again, "produce in us a sense of quiet restfulness, like that which accompanies the consciousness of forgiven sin. They shed abroad the peace of God within our hearts.

"The double reward of kind words is the happiness they cause in others, and the happiness they cause in ourselves. The very process of uttering them is a happiness in itself. Even the imagining of them fills our minds

---

*"Spiritual Conferences," chapter I, section 4.

with sweetness, and makes our hearts glow pleasurably."

We all know that man finds his happiness in his power of action; the more he bestirs himself, the more he enjoys his life. Now, among the different sorts of vital action, it is not ruling over his fellows which makes a man happiest, for there is too much bitterness, there are too many deceptions in the honours to which power entitles us. Neither does the receiving of many gifts from our fellow-men mean that we are supremely happy; flattery and self-interest creep in when gifts have to be given. Rather, then, is it to be truly happy to give oneself unselfishly, to outpour of our best — of the best that is within us. Again, our very best is not our wealth of thought. Hence, to impart knowledge is not the highest happiness of man. Our best is in our hearts, and, as kindness is the virtue which spreads this best abroad, there is no joy to be compared with that of offering to souls thirsting after happiness, of the fulness of a heart overflowing with goodwill to men.

To feel that through us souls have become happier and better is to delight exceedingly; it is as if our life had grown from the adding to it of other happy lives — in the words of Fénelon, "as if one had many lives." "For," as Joubert well remarks, "to our faculties and to our enjoyment, our kindness adds the faculties and the enjoyments of all whom it reaches. Man is immense in his possibility of being, he can exist partially, but his existence is the happier, the more it is complete and full." Goodness, while thus enlarging and multiplying our capability of happiness, our consciousness of being kind, does away with any feeling of uselessness, a feeling which, according to Huxley, "is the worst of the disasters that can befall a man, for if it persists, it results in the atrophy of his every function."

ON KINDNESS

As we shall point out later on, kindness stirs up to new life and develops the whole being of man, setting mind, will, feelings, and above all the heart, to steady work. Many are the emotions which a man experiences, but may not manifest without present danger, or at least without the certainty of future remorse; alone, his kind acts are free to range the wide world over; he need fear from them neither pain nor the bitterness of regret.

You are never quite at ease about a new idea born in your own mind, for you do not know in what storms of contradiction it may involve you. Again, the exercise of your authority over others may provoke rebellion and lead to your overthrow. Your passions are blind, and, if you give them a loose rein, may drag you down to the lowest depths. Kindness alone can trust itself in all security; it leaves peace of conscience behind it in the soul whence it issues, and even if no show of gratitude correspond to it, its essentially pacifying nature can at least stir up no storm. Let us then fearlessly cultivate kindliness of heart, for it is its prerogative to confer happiness unalloyed.

IV

HOW KINDNESS OVERCOMES ALL THINGS

The being at peace with himself and with all the world does not satisfy the heart of man. A deep and imperious unrest urges him on to battle and to conquest. Stifled as it were in the narrow circle of his own personality, he cannot breathe, he cannot fully live, except he push his activity beyond his immediate surroundings — nay, even beyond his own time.

This instinctive need of acting, when dominant in a human heart, creates a conqueror or an apostle. He who is greedy of earthly power may make of a nation his prey; he who burns with love of God and zeal for the salvation of men seeks to master souls.

Even in natures the reverse of energetic, whose every ambition is only too modest, the longing to conquer, to proselytize, is never altogether wanting. Every man, then, should be interested in the delicate art of subjugating his fellows.

Now, to use force is not the best way to conquer; force in some way hurts all that it touches, and as Joubert says, "strength, if it be not applied with kindness, is sure to do some harm."

Brute force can enslave a man; it cannot win him. At the first chance he throws off a yoke which has fettered the body alone and not the heart. Hence, it is not surprising that empires put together by mere force of arms are always ephemeral. Ever true are Christ's words: "The meek shall possess the earth."

THE WORTH OF KINDNESS

Neither does science avail to dominate the will of others. Sometimes it simply dazzles, at others it seems to imprison the mind it addresses, tightly tying it up in the network of its reasonings. Grant that it succeed in mastering the intellect, the heart escapes it. "Man bows before talent; it is at the feet of kindness alone that he freely casts himself down" (Gounod).

The beauty our senses can take note of may captivate the soul; but the emotion it arouses is, strictly speaking, admiration, not love. To move the heart, beauty must have kindliness for its finishing touch. If they be not kindly, neither strength, nor knowledge, nor beauty avail at all to gain lasting victories in the world of souls.

It is because a man feels that he is and ought to be free, that he hates to yield to force, but gives way easily to kindness. On this subject Henry Perreyve has written some beautiful lines, which apostolic men cannot too often ponder: "Christian souls, you who would work as did the Apostles, understand what that earth is which you have resolved to conquer. It is an earth promised to the meek and to none save the meek; for it is a free earth, an intelligent earth, an earth which is its own master, an earth which surrenders to whom it pleases and to him alone, for, as Fénelon said: 'There is no power that can force the inner citadel of the heart.' Nowhere in the Gospel will you find a warrant for the doing of violence to even one single soul, for the disregarding of the honour or of the rights of the least of your fellowmen, nothing to authorize that haughty and assuming tone of voice, those proud and bitter words, or that overbearing and contemptuous manner, by which certain ministers of the Gospel too often think to impress their hearers."

THE WORTH OF KINDNESS

Wherever kindness is the dominant characteristic in a man's dealings with his neighbour, it is sure to make its beneficent influence felt. In all intercourse with others it will insist on courtesy, "that flower of humanity." It will insure peace and good understanding in families, for it makes for constant mutual help, and, in the homely phrase of the proverb, induces everybody "to turn his bristles inwards" (Joubert). We could soothe many sufferings if, as St. Francis of Sales has told us to do, we made of kindness "the first dressing for the wounds which we undertake to heal." Kindness has the secret of correcting faults, for says Joubert, "undue severity freezes them hard and fixes them for good, whereas a wise tolerance will often of itself do away with them. And a good approver is as necessary as a good corrector."

In the educating of the young, kindness is all-powerful; for kind words and kind ways attract children, as surely as harshness repels and represses them. "Away with violence and force," says Montaigne on this point; "so far as I can see, nothing is more apt to debase and to stun a generous nature. My experience is that the use of the rod makes a child cowardly and more than ever maliciously obstinate. I object to any force being used in the education of a tender soul which one is training up to honour and to liberty. There is always something of servility in rigour and constraint, and I maintain that what reason, prudence and tact fail in accomplishing can never be brought about by force."

To children in particular Victor Hugo's maxim applies: "If you want to make men better, make them happier." Such words a preacher of the Gospel may well keep before him. Grace indeed moves the heart interiorly, but outwardly, kindness alone can induce a man voluntarily to embrace a religious belief or determine him to make a moral effort. Other means are sure to fail.

"It is not possible," says St. Vincent of Paul, "that we preachers should bring forth good fruits, if we, like barren soil, only produce thistles; there must be in us something attractive, something pleasant, or we shall repel everyone." "If we come forward in the likeness of ravening wolves," says in his turn St. John Chrysostom, "we are sure to be beaten." Goodness, on the contrary, never fails to win souls. "The very convicts," says St. Vincent of Paul, "amongst whom I lived can be gained over; and in no other way. When I spoke sharply to them I spoilt everything, and on the contrary, when I praised them for being resigned to their hard lot and pitied their sufferings; when I kissed their chains, and showed that I felt for them, then they listened to me, then they gave glory to God, and then they sought to put themselves into a state of grace."

In the apostle of Christ, kindness, besides its innate attractiveness, is a kind of visible demonstration of the truth of religion; it seems to present all problems ready solved.

Dumas tersely but very clearly sets forth this apologetic value of goodness: "Not even genius avails to explain what God is; but the kindness of men is a proof that He is." And that angelic soul Madame Swetchine, who herself by sheer force of kindness ruled so many, expresses herself admirably: "The practice of virtues, lovable virtues, is the sole language of faith that can inspire any respect for religion in unbelieving or all but unbelieving minds. Hence we are wrong, and very wrong, in not preaching God in the only manner in which He can be understood." And she adds: "If good people were kinder people, there would not be so many sinners." The conclusion we may put as St. John Chrysostom puts it: "Throw the net of charity, bait it with kindness. Remain always a lamb and you will always be a conqueror."

In setting forth the excellency of kindness we have shown that alone it makes the kind man perfectly happy: that alone it conquers the souls of men and makes an apostleship fruitful. Truly Montaigne was right when he insisted that "every other science is hurtful to him who is not versed in the science of goodwill to his fellow-men." And with him we may add: "Even if I could make myself feared, I had far rather make myself loved."

Chapter II

ON THE NATURE OF TRUE KINDNESS

THOUGH a virtuous soul is naturally inclined to be kind, and though kindness of all virtues is the easiest to practise without being taught, we will nevertheless here set down in order its characteristics, partly in order to make it to be more loved by making it better known; partly to help the kindhearted to use some sort of method in carrying out the suggestions of their own good nature.

The first of all acts of kindness is to pity any who suffer; a heart moved by the pain of another straightway feels itself instinctively drawn to succour him in his trouble. But the gifts of the kind man must be given kindly, graciously, else the kind act will be no balm to the soul of the sufferer. But the supreme act of Christian kindness, and the most a man can give to his fellow, is to love him as himself.

There are, therefore, varying degrees of kindness; and the more precious the gift it bestows, the more perfect it is in itself. When merely compassionate, it gives pity; when actively beneficent, it sacrifices money, goods, time, and comfort; when gracious in the practical expression of its compassion, it bears witness that it respects and honours those on whom it confers favours; when, in fine, it is, in Scriptural phrase, *loving,* kindness means the giving to another of one's very heart.

I

HOW TRUE KINDNESS IS COMPASSIONATE

"It is only pity that can make us kind," says Joubert. At any rate, to feel for others is the first and surest proof of a kind heart. Look neither for devotedness nor for sympathy from a heart that the sight of pain does not touch.

There are men and women who take no notice of the sufferings of others. Every day they see people in trouble; but it neither surprises them nor affects them; they would not think of stopping to help up again a poor man who has fallen down, nor to aid in dressing the gaping wounds of one whom some accident has stricken to death. They simply pass on, nor allow the trouble of their neighbour to draw them for a single instant from their pursuit of pleasure or from their business. Nothing will they sacrifice for the sake of their suffering fellow-creatures. It is of such as these one is thinking when one speaks of hard, cold, callous hearts.

Again, there are men and women who, in presence of acute distress, forget to pity the sufferer, so intent are

THE NATURE OF TRUE KINDNESS

they on discovering where the fault lies. They seem to be seeking to know the truth in order that they may feel justified in shutting compassionateness out of their hearts and in trampling on those who have fallen, rather than reach out to them a helping hand; they make known weaknesses of others about which they would do well to be silent, and take a truly criminal pleasure in fatally compromising by their indiscreet utterances persons whom a charitable silence might have saved. Of a truth, the hearts of such as these are evil.

The impulses of a kind heart are quite other. By a mysterious instinct it seems to become conscious of distress; no detail of pain escapes it, it pierces any and every poor cloak with which shame may seek to hide wretchedness. Far from turning away from the sight of suffering as from something that revolts, the man of kind heart cannot refrain from gazing upon what only makes him long the more to stay and help. He does not trouble to blame the unfortunate; he knows only how to commiserate them, to suffer with them, above all to understand them.

For him, a fault is atoned for by the mere fact that it is suffered for. Indeed, a truly kind heart cannot heed the fault; it sees only the consequent misery; and this is the very reason why the pity of the truly kindhearted is so sweet to all who mourn.

To the kind man every sort of trouble appeals; bodily pain, sadness of heart, the wounds one's surroundings or one's bad fortune has inflicted, mental suffering—for such there surely is — nay, peradventure is pain of mind the hardest of all to bear.

The kind man never makes little of another's real sufferings; his heart all but bleeds for the least of them. He concerns himself, too, about sorts of distress concerning which people, as a rule, do not trouble; the everyday, commonplace woe of artisans employed in unhealthy workshops, of women subsisting on starvation wages, of children left to roam the streets, or, though mere babies, already worked to death. Secretly the kind heart feeds the shamefaced poor; very noticeably it shows respect for and honours all whom the world scorns; on the forsaken and desolate it lavishes its words of comfort and encouragement.

Nor can there ever be a lack of opportunities for the kind heart to show itself as such. "The poor you have always with you," said Christ. These words are always true, however much and well men have worked in our time for the bettering of the lot of the masses.

Let civilization be advanced as it may, always will there be orphans to succour, the helplessly sick to look after, the feeble-minded to protect, the weak-willed and tempted to watch over, the listless and incapable to be kept up and pushed on. The world will never be without men on the point of making shipwreck of their lives, not without women ready to sacrifice to vanity the well-being of their homes. The ambitious or sensual man will always put the gratifying of his unlawful desires above duty. The uncurbed passions of the criminal will always as now be a danger to society.

Hospitals and refuges may be enlarged, dispensaries and industrial schools multiplied, prisons and labour colonies better organized; misery will not disappear from our streets; you will find it on your own doorstep, and sooner than let go its hold on you, it will attack you yourself and find its way into your very heart.

In presence of this inevitable suffering, albeit convinced that there needs must always be suffering about it, the compassionate heart never wearies; day after day distress appeals to it, moves it, as if there were always novelty in pain. It is attracted by suffering, not from reason or duty, nor because it has made a business of charity, not even (apart from what is supernatural) to fulfil the Will of God — high as this last motive is — but because it is a human being that suffers.

"Kindness," says Lacordaire, "is a virtue that does not think about its own interest; does not wait for the call of duty; has no need of æsthetic attraction to solicit it; but is instinctively the more drawn towards its object, the more that object is wretched, poor, forsaken, and, humanly speaking, contemptible."

Any so-called kindness not springing from this natural feeling of compassion will inevitably be hard and austere; it may perhaps be self-sacrificing, but it can never attract.

No heart can be as tender in its compassion as is the Heart of Christ. For in this Sacred Heart, which is one thing with the mercy of God, began upon earth the reign of pity. Infinite were its riches, but of them all Christ willed to make manifest only His goodwill to man. Pitying all, hard on none, Christ understood and solaced every suffering. They brought the sick to Him and He healed them; He met lepers and He cleansed them; He saw the dead wept over and He raised them to life; He multiplied the loaves to feed the multitudes that had followed Him into the wilderness; Magdalen's tears He did not spurn; at His feet the woman taken in adultery found forgiveness and salvation; He was moved by Peter's tears, and He heard the prayer of the penitent thief. His dying in shame on the Cross that we might be saved was a supreme act of pity for us.

He taught His disciples to be kind — to be kind always. To those who would have had Him call down fire from heaven on the ungrateful city of

THE NATURE OF TRUE KINDNESS

Samaria, His one reply was: "Ye know not of what spirit you are." What His spirit was He has taught us in the parable of the good Samaritan, who, going down from Jerusalem to Jericho, and lighting upon a man sore wounded, stayed on his way to pour the oil and wine of his charity into the poor traveller's open wounds, and to have him cared for at his benefactor's charge in the nearest inn.

Christ condemned the hardhearted in the person of Dives, who, seated at a sumptuous table, had no thought of Lazarus dying of hunger on his threshold, and cast the remains of his banquet to the dogs, utterly heedless of the poor. In fine, He warns us that God's mercy is for the merciful, and for the merciful alone.

The Saints have each one largely shared in the charity of Christ, but the character of St. Vincent of Paul seems to have been above that of others its living expression. There is not a single form of human misery by which, at some time or another in his life, the heart of this Saint was not moved. The destitute, the sick, forsaken children, victims of war and of famine, galley-slaves, prisoners, hardened criminals, women in trouble or in danger, all alike moved him to pity, all were lovingly helped by him. True as pretty are the prints of the time that picture him gathering up forsaken children from the streets of Paris, and himself carrying them to the homes he had got ready for them.

He was not a philosopher who has argued out the duty of every man to take his share of a joint responsibility; it was simply that he was holy and human, and that he was touched to the heart by the sufferings of others.

He himself says as much: "Oh, Madam, what a harvest there is to gather for heaven, particularly in these days when the misery at our very doors is so great.... I am anxious for the future of our Congregation, yet most truly I can say that it does not trouble me nearly so much as does the lot of the poor; we priests can always ask bread from those among ourselves who have it, or we can disperse and work as parish priests in different parts of the country; but my poor, what can they do? Where can they go? Now you know what really is my burden, my sorrow."

Now, this compassionateness for which the sufferings of the poor are "a burden and a sorrow," can it be acquired by everyone? Its germ is surely implanted in each individual soul; for, as Bossuet remarks: "When God made the heart of man, the first thing He implanted in it was kindness." Nevertheless, in too many hearts this germ has dried up. Nor must we be surprised if we meet with many men and women hard and insensible to the sufferings of others. In certain highly gifted natures the God-implanted seed of kindliness may grow of itself, but in most hearts it needs cultivation to force it into healthy life and action. Therefore, it is that it is important to begin early to teach children to be kind and compassionate. In the words of a writer of our own time, "Men have more need to be taught how to pity the sufferings of others than how to bear their own."

II

HOW TRUE KINDNESS IS GENEROUS

"Good impulses are just nothing at all unless they develop into good actions." This remark of a thinker is not altogether true, for the mere pity felt by a kind heart may be itself a kind deed. All sufferers are helped by feeling themselves understood, thought about and sympathized with. Of the manifold miseries which we meet on our path through life, only a small number can call for sacrifice and devotedness on our part; but all claim at least our compassion. Tears of sympathy are never shed in vain; they heal the wounds that caused them to flow.

But to pity is, after all, only to begin to do good; of its very nature kindness tends to express itself by means of kind and charitable actions. The human heart, when deeply moved, is an overfull vessel; it cannot contain the torrent of goodness that wells up within it. And Father Faber has very truly laid down that "kindness is the overflowing of self upon others." The heart that is moved by compassion makes the sufferings of others its own; it grieves over them; it weeps over them; it tries to relieve them. To still the cry of pain it sacrifices everything — time, money, trouble, its very existence. It would give anything to be able to do away with the suffering which at the moment is before it, and to realize its own noble ambition to add a measure of justice and happiness to the world's history.

The compassionate heart gives of its time. Do the duties of its state leave it any leisure? Such leisure is hoarded like a precious treasure, not that therewith one may yield to the allurements of pleasure nor for the profit of business, but that it may be devoted to the service of the poor and the afflicted, or may be spent in paying visits of charity, or in working for the distressed. In a word, that it may be taken up with the saying of kind words and with the doing of kind actions.

This was the lesson taught by St. Vincent of Paul to the Ladies of Charity, and later by Ozanam to the young students whom he gathered to his conferences. Those who treasure up the smallest fragments of their time as so much precious coin and spend them on the poor, are blessed of God surely as much as they who give to the needy their cast-off garments and what remains from their table. But the compassionate man gives also of his money. Once such necessary expenditure as is required by his station in life has been met, what is over he carefully sets aside for the benefit of those who are in want. If he is well-to-do, he draws upon his superfluous riches with a lavish hand, only too happy to be able to relieve a greater number of the needy.

There are more people in the world than one would think who practise the strictest economy for the sole purpose of enabling themselves to follow the generous inclinations of their kind hearts, without, in so doing, omitting any expenditure proper to their station in life. There are, everywhere, humble working girls and poor labourers who, like the widow praised in the Gospel, take day by day from the little they have their mite for the hungry and the homeless.

Besides time and money, the kind man gives to his suffering fellow-men of his strength, of his talents, of all his resources. He takes pains to be kind. He does not mind trouble; after emptying his purse he spends himself.

There are kind people who make clothes for the poor, others artistic or useful objects to be sold for their benefit; others again who visit and tend the sick in their poor homes.

Not all the "Little Sisters" who go forth into the by-ways of our cities to comfort the suffering wear a coif; God only knows how much devotedness is the more effectually hidden by a worldly dress, and how often dainty hands are discreetly employed in her service by holy Charity, in making beds, in washing children, or in cooking humble meals.

In other walks of life this selfsame kindliness of heart takes all manner of trouble — faces perhaps even humiliations, to get employment for a man out of work, to save a woman in trouble from utter ruin, or to retrieve from wretchedness and dishonour one of the many lives of agony hidden away under a commonplace exterior.

Again, in a higher and more special sense, the sympathetic heart truly gives to others its very self. It clings to those whom it helps. What it is kind to, that will it first respect, and eventually love. Likely enough, it will receive neither gratitude nor love in return, nevertheless in the end it needs must love those to whom it does good. Even when, in the words of St. Paul, "for loving more he himself is the less loved" (II Cor. xii. 15), the kind man does not lose heart, for of true affection as of all else, "verily is it more blessed to give than to receive." The virtue of kindliness pushed thus far has reached its perfection.

Unselfishness is the first condition for the bestowing of a benefit to be a true act of kindness. The master who in ancient times looked after the health and well-being of his slaves, but only in order that they might work the better for him, had not the merit of charity, because he was seeking his own interest and nothing besides; in the same way, he who rendering a service to another looks upon it simply as a good investment, out of which he hopes for profit, neither acts from kindness nor feels the joy that is brought by the doing of a kind act; such a one may be a good man of business, but not necessarily kind-hearted. The kind man is no calculator. He asks for nothing from the gift he bestows except the joy of having helped misfortune. He has no thought of material advantage, or of praise which may accrue to him from being kind. He purposely envelops his best actions in silence and secludedness; far from himself proclaiming them with self-satisfied pride, he conceals them as carefully as others hide their faults;

THE NATURE OF TRUE KINDNESS

he wants the world to know nothing at all of his good deeds, and even the poor to benefit by them without feeling that they owe them to him. He tries "not to let his left hand know what his right hand doeth." Hence, he prefers those good deeds which are ordinary to those which are striking; and for the very reason that good done at home has mostly the look of a duty, and rarely implies an out-of-the-way devotedness, he puts in the foremost place those acts of self-denial by which his own household benefits. To be the less noticed he likes to give his life, so to speak, piecemeal. So little does he look for gratitude that if by chance it comes to him it surprises him. For, ever there ring in his ears those words of Christ: "When you shall have done all these things that are commanded, you say: We are unprofitable servants; we have done that which we ought to do."

Kindness must not only be unselfish, it must be catholic. The truly kindhearted man knows no acceptation of persons in the distributing of what he has to give. He considers himself beholden to all sufferers.

The kindliness of the Jews was limited to their brethren according to the flesh, the children of Abraham; they hated the rest of mankind. Christian kindliness reveals its divine origin in that it extends to every creature. According even to Schopenhauer: "When kindness dwells in a heart, it opens that heart wide enough for it to embrace the whole world."

Kindness makes no distinctions on account either of nationalities, or of opinions, or of sympathies, or of antipathies; wherever it sees misery, there it speeds. "I meet," writes Jules Simon, "a poor man who is suffering from hunger. I hasten to relieve him. What does his name or his country matter? I shall never see him again; but he is a man.... The Sister of Charity takes the habit of St. Vincent of Paul and enters a hospital: whom is she going to look after, comfort and heal? She has no idea — some human being or other. All who need her care are sure of her welcome. This is love of mankind."

The wicked, even, are not excluded from the solicitous tenderness of the truly kind, for as Plato remarked: "If they are forsaken by their fellow-men, they can but become more wicked." And here God Himself vouchsafes to set us the example: "Does He not make His sun to rise on the just and on the unjust?" Has not Jesus Christ atoned for the sins of all mankind? And has not that eloquent preacher of the Master's doctrine, St. Paul, declared that for Christians "there is no distinction between Jew and Gentile, Greek and Roman, Scythian and Barbarian, for that all men are brethren in Christ Jesus"? The distinctive note of Christian charity would be wanting in our kindliness if our motive in being kind were other than that of wishing to do good to someone just because he is our fellow-man.

Yet charity must not be practised without discernment. On the contrary, charity should be intelligent, and far from blindly distributing the means at its disposal, should increase the value of its gifts by the opportuneness of its bestowing of them. In some cases an almsdeed means the giving of money in place of help in other forms. The assistance required by those whom infirmity renders unfit for work differs from the aid to be bestowed on men and women in distress but able to earn their own living.

True kindness is fully conscious that alms are hurtful if they unduly dispense a man from taking his part in the struggle to live; it is, therefore, ingenious in seeking out the work for which each one is fit; for artisans according to their trade and skill, for

THE NATURE OF TRUE KINDNESS

boys and girls the means of learning the one and acquiring the other. It is more really kind and a far truer act of charity to spur the able-bodied on to work than to relieve their distress temporarily by the gift of money.

Similarly, in the matter of education, it is true kindness to let the child off no work, to insist on its own individual effort. Only by urging the child to act for itself can its character be developed and fitted for the battle of life.

It is deplorable that the rich seem to prefer to put unquestioningly considerable sums into the hands of the poor, rather than to follow the needy step by step and to take the trouble to show them how to help themselves. A wise foresight, a taking into account of any probable outcome of his kind act, is essential to the kind man; and no one wishful to be kind must forget it.

Lastly, almsgiving is the expression of true Christian charity only when it respects the dignity and the feelings of the poor. One meets at times with men who give away a great deal of money, but whose harshness is painful, even insulting, to those whom they help. Their very favours are made to be a burden hard to bear. True kindliness is considerate and discreet; it inspires a delicate mode of treating with the poor which conciliates them and respects both their feelings and their freedom.

In giving alms, beware of wounding the pride of the poor: do not humble still more a man whose misery already lowers him enough in his own eyes; do not let him imagine that you are lording it over him; efface yourself for sheer fear of offending him. On this condition only can you again make of an outcast — a man and a friend.

Remember that, needy though he be, the poor man is a free man. It is bad

THE NATURE OF TRUE KINDNESS

enough for him to be tyrannized over by misfortune, or by the brute forces of nature; do not, by exacting what he need not give, crush the man who feels himself to be a failure. Do not make his chains heavier; rather set him quite free, so that he may the more surely become better. It may be that the respect you show will not be appreciated by all the poor, but it is certain that the charity which is overbearing always irritates and at the same time depresses them. The most Christian and the greatest benefactors of the poor are assuredly those who strive to hide their own better fortune, and to bridge over the distance between the poor and themselves. By showing itself retiring, almost shy, their generosity clothes itself with the winning charm of true kindliness.

III

HOW TRUE KINDNESS IS GRACIOUS

"When thou givest, give gladly, give with a smile." Long before Joubert, St. Paul had expressed the same thought: "God loveth a cheerful giver." The pleasant smile with which kindheartedness enhances the good deeds it does is called graciousness. A gracious act is essentially a kind act, and it is one of greater value than the mere expenditure of time, toil, or money, for not content with giving without stint its goods, in very truth it puts its own life into its gifts.

Graciousness has two advantages over mere almsgiving. First, there are many of our fellow-creatures who have no need of our money, but there is not one of all those with whom we have to deal to whom our sympathy is not good and precious; so that, though by our very liberality we run the risk of wounding the pride of some, our graciousness has the privilege of rejoicing the hearts of all.

Secondly, there is something dry and haughty about the mere bestowing of money; it is graciousness which makes our almsdeeds look natural, unaffected and pleasing. For surely the poverty which you relieve calls for your tact in dealing with it quite as much as for your alms; the needy hunger for rejoicing of heart as much as they do for bread, and all food nourishes the better for being, so to speak, steeped in joy.

Were a Sister of Charity, however skilful her hands, to do no more than dress the wounds of the body, she would only have performed half of her task; it is equally her vocation to endeavour to heal the wounds of the soul, by the kind and gracious words she utters.

Graciousness, then, is like a finishing touch given to the beauty of charity; it is the salt without which almsgiving loses its savour.

Graciousness does not consist in the empty civility of manners outwardly pleasing. It has its seat in the inmost soul, and the engaging smile it places on the lips is only the faithful reflection of the kind thoughts with which the heart is overflowing. Graciousness springs from an interior feeling of esteem for the person on whom one bestows a favour; did such esteem not exist, an approving smile would be but a deceptive mask. To be genuine, our gracious ways must be the echo of the praise resounding within the inner sanctuary of our being of Him to whom we are thus gracious.

Graciousness of thought is far more rare and far more difficult than graciousness of word or graciousness of action. It is the great gift of thinking of others without criticizing them and without despising them. Nor to its possession can we attain without much effort; for, in order to soften our thoughts in their very origin, and by so doing to correct the bitterness of our judgments, we must conquer that natural tendency which leads us all to find out and to tell others of the weak points in our neighbour's character. St. Francis of Sales never showed more clearly how wonderfully kind he was than when he said that if a matter had a hundred bad sides and only one good one, it was the good side he would look at. His surpassing delicacy of feeling led him to put a favourable interpretation upon everything, and that secret indulgence which men reserve for the regarding of their own faults was St. Francis's invariable characteristic in thinking about the shortcomings of others.

Some will say that to believe in and talk about good intentions when evildoing is scandalous, is mere folly; but does not each one of us, strong in the warrant of his own conscience, in the name of justice as well as in that of charity, claim to have his rectitude of intention recognized and respected? What right have we to be hard on others, we who exact that so many allowances be made in our own case?

Being, too, so eager to find excuses for ourselves, how is it that we are so ready to accuse other people? We may disapprove of an action, and may say so, but we need not judge and condemn the doer. If in your heart you think ill of your brother, your protestations of attachment to him are essentially false, and your words must needs lack that accent of sympathy which truth alone can impart. If, on the contrary, you think the best of all, and, trustful of the uprightness of the intentions of others, show yourself indulgent to their weaknesses, you have only to follow the bent of your feel-

THE NATURE OF TRUE KINDNESS

ings to show unmistakable kindness in word and in action.

Lacordaire has remarked truly that kind thoughts stamp themselves on the features with a beauty which attracts souls.

Graciousness does away alike with the sullenness which repels and the indifference which freezes. Not only does it impart that exquisite courtesy of manner which Joubert rightly styles "the flower of that plant which is man"; it diffuses over one's whole personality an indefinable something which warms, vivifies and attracts. Often and often on meeting a person we realize instinctively whether his thoughts are kind or the reverse. Strive as we may, a man cannot utterly shut up his soul within him. Whether we will or no, it escapes, it manifests itself; it creates around us an atmosphere which betrays our genuine feelings. From kind hearts there flow, as it were, sympathetic currents, the beneficent influences of which are felt more quickly and reach much farther than words or deeds.

It is very sure that the tongue soon becomes the ready servant of a kind mind. No one need fear that a man of feeling will say aught to embitter or to humble another, or to make him fall into that mood of utter wretchedness which is more fatal to mankind than dagger or poison. On the contrary, sympathetic words have for the listener's soul a healing virtue which calms suffering, and a nourishing virtue which calls back the joy of living and braces to cheerful work.

The kind man takes heed lest he wound by oversharply criticizing or by indulging in witticisms, clever maybe, but galling beyond belief for him who is their butt. He does not make fun of his neighbour; but, on the contrary, knows very well how, tactfully and without flattering, to praise where praise is deserved. He is careful never

THE NATURE OF TRUE KINDNESS

in conversing with another to recall any painful memory, but instinctively and quite unaffectedly talks, and makes others talk, of things pleasant, wholesome and in some way or other uplifting. He has a softening way about him, and without perceiving it himself, brings people to make up their quarrels, and however touchy they may be, to keep the peace. Even those whom Nicole calls the "miserable all around," a kindly man's genial talk as it were galvanizes into at least momentary cheerfulness. It was by sweet and gentle speech that Christ won over the multitudes to Himself, and that later on His disciples conquered the world.

Kindheartedness, in fine, lends an indefinable charm to our actions. Watch the daily dealings of a man who is thoroughly good-hearted. He is affable to all who come across him; he never lets people suspect that he is tired of them and of their talk. He listens patiently to wearisome accounts of other people's woes, and refuses to get angry on hearing for the hundredth time one and the same complaint; for he feels that he lightens many burdens by letting the unhappy insist upon telling him of the unexampled hardship of their misfortunes, and of the unjustifiable deceptions they have experienced. He thankfully accepts services of which he has no need, to allow others to enjoy the sense of being kind to him. He does not think at all about his own pleasures or even interests; his thoughts refuse to be self-centred; all his preoccupation and all his solicitude is for the well-being of others. His watchful considerateness gives him marvellous intuition; he feels instinctively what will displease, and avoids it; he recognizes on the instant what will please, and does it. Whenever there is question of sparing pain or of giving pleasure' he counts the cost of no sacrifice, whether of money, of time or of self. His kindheartedness has come to be

THE NATURE OF TRUE KINDNESS

far more than a mere good-natured wish to help; it dares everything.

Goodwill to others surrounds a soul of which it is the life, with the most stimulating of atmospheres; it is a very fount of peace, joy and strength.

Nothing so surely takes away one's peace of mind as the knowing oneself to be thought little of; of all human sufferings, humiliation is the most keenly felt. Scorn, whether betrayed by manner or put into humbling words, or manifested by contemptuous treatment, is fatal where it wounds, save for him who has learned from Christian faith to care not at all for the judgments of men, and to be content with the good testimony rendered him by God in his own conscience.

But few of us have grown to this. We feel like the rest of men; like them we cannot help caring; when humbled, we are inevitably cast down. Kind words, and a show of respect and sympathy, are the medicine we want in our trouble. Put us where we can feel we are understood and thought well of, and forthwith we get our spirits back and are well again.

For men and women, indeed, who in the literal sense are saints, it may suffice that God makes them feel in prayer that He knows them, that He approves them, and that He blesses them; but for all who are still trammelled by usual human weaknesses, tranquillity of soul only comes back when those whom they look up to as sincere and enlightened, show themselves kind and sympathetic. There is no occasion, then, to be sparing of kind words, of words that spell peace to our fellow-men. Cheerfulness is the outcome of peace of heart.

A truly kind action, for the very reason that it implies some sort of esteem and affection for a sufferer, not only tranquillizes his mind, but cheers his whole being. As rays of health-bringing sunlight, dispelling the darkness of a wretched hovel, so is the smile of the kind-hearted in the gloom of the troubled heart.

Of far more price than the food and assiduous care the Little Sisters of the Poor lavish on the old people entrusted to them, is the ray of joy their own kindly cheerfulness sheds on the evening of sorely tried lives.

Would that worldly women, who waste in silly goings to and fro, or in tasteless pleasures, the time which they complain hangs so heavily on their hands, did but know the worth to the poor of a cheering word, and the happiness that one may feel in uttering it! Possibly they would spend something, not only of their time and money, but of their winningness of manner and of their cheerful talk, on their sisters in sore distress.

Again, cheerfulness is good for us morally, for it strengthens the will, and by so doing, braces all the other energies of the soul. As we have already said, it is hard to be virtuous when we are not happy; and hard to work when we feel listless and cast down. Here it is that the glory of kindness comes in. It makes people better because it makes them brighter. It implies esteem and so restores confidence. It cheers, and so is the best stimulus to work. As Madame Swetchine says: "Let us never stop scattering seeds of kindness and of sympathy along our way. No doubt many seeds will be lost, but if there be but one which springs up, it will be as a fragrance on all our path, and an unceasing joy to our hearts."

And yet she has not said all. For with the enjoyment of life which our kind acts assure us, there must be reckoned the fruitfulness of these same lives of ours, whether we be looked upon as social workers or as Christian apostles. And, on the other hand, to sum up, if it be true that the kind man, because of his very kindness, leads a life more intense, and therefore more enjoyable, than that of others, it must be likewise true that to dissuade a man from doing a kind action is to try to kill the best of the life that is in him.

IV

HOW TRUE KINDNESS IS LOVING

Kindness is more than gracious; it is loving. A kind heart loves those to whom it does good, and the love it bestows is above every other of its gifts. Kindness may begin in mere pity with words of sympathy; the more it grows the more it leads to the doing of kind and generous actions, to the bestowing on the needy at the cost of self-denial; gracious ways are its fragrant flowers; the peace, joy and strength it bestows are its sweet and welcome fruit; but it is in the gift of itself by love for him whom it succours that it is truly perfected. Only to those whom a man loves as Christ willed we should love our neighbour, does a man really throw open the inner sanctuary of his being, and offer the holiest of his treasures, his affection.

Nor before this has come to pass can kindness use to the full its power of conquest, for, says Lacordaire: "God has willed that no good should be done to man unless the gift be sanctified by love; and that heartlessness should forever be incapable either of imparting light or of inspiring virtue."

Nevertheless, it is most true that love is a feeling which cannot be forced upon us; neither from our fellow-men, nor even from our own selves, will our hearts accept coercion; rather, the more we are urged to feel affectionate, the more we draw back, for to do aught otherwise than freely is unnatural to man.

If, then, on the one hand, to be good to all is a precept, and if, on the other hand, to force ourselves to feel affection for all is beyond our power, we must necessarily make some distinction between being kind and being affectionate, and must admit that there can be a true kindness of heart which is not loving, and that it is possible to be compassionate, generous and gracious without feeling any natural affection for the person to whom we are kind.

We express very different feelings when we say: "I love such a one as much as I ought to love him, and as fully as charity requires of me," and when we simply say: "I love him." Assuredly, to fulfil our whole duty to our fellow-man is Christian charity, but to be spurred on by God-given affection to the doing of our whole duty, and of more than our whole duty, is charity made perfect.

Yet, after all, the distance between kindness and love is not great. Love involves kindness. We cannot begin to love without beginning to be kind; where our heart goes our whole being follows. Our neighbour, when loved, becomes dear to us as ourselves; his sufferings move us as if they were our very own; his needs call insistently for all we have to give; he holds, perforce, a high place in our esteem, and almost involuntarily we are lavish in regard to him of respect and of all manner of delicate attentiveness.

Kindness on its side leads to love. Its first act, pity, implies a beginning of love; in proportion as it prompts to the sacrifice of time and means, the kind heart surely follows what it gives. We begin by being kind; we end by loving those to whom we are kind.

An African missionary will show you, without meaning to, that he positively loves his Negroes; a Brother of St. John of God, his feeble-minded and feeble-bodied incurables; a Lady of Calvary, her cancer patients. Father Damien literally loved his lepers. Utter self-sacrifice of such sort invariably finds in the love which makes it easy its crown, its joy and its earthly reward.

More than this, devotedness finds that, if to be loved is good, to love is better. If there be benefactors who have no kindly feeling for those whom they make indebted to them, it is that such benefactors give rather to please themselves than to do good to their fellow-creatures; they have given money from their purses, but they have given nothing from their hearts; had it been true kindliness that inspired and guided them in what they did, needs must but they would love those whose benefactors they are.

It is the goodness to others which springs from genuine affection that Holy Scripture praises when it teaches us: "A faithful friend is a strong defence, and he that hath found him hath found a treasure." It was goodness like to this that a poor man, who was a deep thinker, claimed when he called as of right for "Not alms, but friends!" And the Eastern proverb, again, is right in advising us "not to let the grass grow on the path of friendship." For friendship truly peoples the dreary solitude of a lonely soul; it dispels the sadness inevitable where no comforting word is heard; it in some way binds up, if it cannot always heal, the wounds of those who in the battle of life have gone under. The value of true friendship is that of Christian kindliness, of Christian charity, for which friendship is but another name.

"Woe to him that is alone," and "It is not good for man to be alone." These are Divinely inspired words, and all human experience shows how true they are. The talents of the man who stands alone, a few exceptions apart, are barren; there is no one to rouse him to action, to hearten him and push him on, to keep him from slackening and probably soon giving up out of sheer, dull weariness. The friendless man is timid, unenterprising, easily frightened off. "Fear," writes Lamennais, "dogs the footsteps of the man who makes his way apart from his friends — it sits beside him when he rests, nor leaves him even when he sleeps." Men who lead habitually lonely lives mostly become the prey of their own imagination — any and every trifling discomfort is a torture for them, their oversensitiveness is on edge, excruciating to themselves; they suspect everybody, and for that very reason are helplessly miserable.

We know, of course, that there are happy and fruitful solitudes; solitudes where genius meditates its masterpieces; solitudes where silent prayer strengthens sin-weakened wills; solitudes where souls, worn out by the work of the world, seek and find a rest that heals and renews. We know, too, that the man who does not know how to help himself with an occasional hour of silence and serious thought will likely enough quickly break down under the stress and toil of life. But it is not of wholesome solitude that we are now speaking.

It is to a heart dead to human affection that solitude is hurtful.

One can live far from the haunts of men without being, in the non-Christian sense of the word, a solitary — witness the Carthusian monk in his cell. And one can live in the bustle of a great city, jostling one's fellows all the day long, and yet feel within one's empty heart the cruel dreariness of solitude; numberless men and women live miserably alone in the very heart of society. One can live a lonely life, and an unhappy one because of its loneliness, in the midst of an outwardly united family circle—nay, even in the quietest of religious homes.

Loneliness of heart is a mysterious and painful malady, which the sufferer almost instinctively conceals. The distress it inevitably causes is far more severe in some cases than in others; it seems to be keener in proportion as education and culture have rendered the soul more sensitive to mental pain.

Ordinarily speaking, a man cannot by himself find relief from the suffering consequent on interior loneliness. The giving oneself up to wilful misanthropy does not take away the pain the lonely man feels; it inevitably aggravates it.

It is most true that for certain chosen souls the strength of their religious faith at once fills up the void in their hearts, by making them see God present within themselves. But there are comparatively few souls so entirely detached from what is created, as to be, in the sense of the Saints, satisfied with God alone; God Himself, oftener than not, is pleased neither comfortingly to visit nor persistently to sustain the souls of men, except by using their fellow-creatures as His instrument.

The man who has not acquaintances only, but friends, is no longer alone in the world. His heart ceases to be an empty house; he finds that, without knowing it, he is not bored as before with everything, that life is enjoyable; and he begins to want to be useful. His time does not, as before, hang heavily and purposelessly on his hands; on the contrary, no day is long enough for the man who basks in the warm sunshine of friendship. It has been well said that "every friendless life is hopelessly incomplete"; for it is the love and goodwill of his fellowmen that gives fulness to the life of a man.

Happy, then, are they who on their way meet with true friendship: let them take heed lest they close their door against it, and let them welcome it like a kind genie to their hearts and homes! But yet happier are they whose goodwill to all makes of their every neighbour a friend. Veritable saviours of souls are they, for through them the wilderness blossoms, and the barren lives of the forsaken bring forth a rich and gladdening harvest.

Let him who has entered on the path of kindliness go on fearlessly to the end; mere philanthropy, if harsh, humiliates in helping; sympathetic talk, if cold, is like a far-off light, too faint for us to see by its glimmer that for every life there is joy and hope: and never let the kind man forget that Christian kindness must be lovingkindness, else it would not be human; and it would not be the healing of the ills of life.

Our faith teaches us how Christ saved us, and saves us, by love; and, in the hands of apostolic men, that kindness which is affectionate and which does not conceal its affectionateness, is an all-powerful weapon. While it rescues hearts from their own loneliness, lifting them, as it were, bodily out of the slough of discouragement and kindling anew their will to live, it wins them over to the longing for a yet higher life. For, conquered by a kindness unmistakably God-inspired, they turn instinctively to Him. Kindliness is His very breath, and this they feel it to be.

Pascal once said, "It is the heart, not the reason, which feels God." No preacher can make human reason grasp the truth unless by kindness the seed has beforehand been sown in the hearts of his hearers.

Chapter III

ON THE WAY TO BECOME KIND

I

HOW THE SORT OF MIND A MAN HAS LEADS TO HIS BEING KIND-HEARTED OR OTHERWISE

IT IS obvious that kindness is not a mere mental gift. Yet to imagine with some that kindness of disposition in no way depends upon intellectual ability, much more to hold that clever people cannot be expected to be kind, is a very great mistake.

The intellect, it is sometimes observed, can descant learnedly upon the nature of kindness, but cannot impart it; talent means brilliancy and clearness of understanding, whereas kindliness is warmth of heart — a very different thing. An overkeen insight into what we see of our fellow-men seems even to shut the door upon kindness. The clever man's sharp reply, witty though it be, to an appeal for sympathy and help, mostly hurts more than his money or advice relieves; it is only from simple and unassuming thoughts that there flow the kind words and kind deeds which are as healing balm to wounds.

Whatever of truth there may be in this, we hold that there is a kind mind as there is a kind heart; and that kind thoughts, kind words and kind deeds are, in general, naturally inseparable and dependent each one on the others. For it is the mind that shows the heart where, and how, and why to be kind. It is the mind that frees the heart from the groundless fears and foolish suspicions that act as a drag upon its kindly impulses; while, in return, the heart softens the mind and makes it kind.

Many others before us have insisted on the debt a man's heart owes to his understanding. Comte writes: "Every noble intellectual flight leads of its very nature and directly to a feeling of sympathy with mankind." Gaston Davenay puts it that "the heart" (by which he means kindheartedness) "is nobility of intellect in one of its most beautiful forms." Another psychological writer affirms that, "though it be possible to be kind without being clever, no one can be very clever without becoming very kind."

This remark is, moreover, a very ancient one, since in the Old Testament the wise man exhorts us "to *understand* our neighbour," and the Psalmist calls "blessed" the man who *understands* the poor and the needy, as if the fact of understanding distress brought in its train the doing of all acts of goodwill to our fellow-men.

Truly, too, there is no little merit in getting to understand a man, that most complex of beings, and more especially a man who is suffering.

Looked at merely from the outside, man appears to be "uneven and changeable," many-sided and self-contradictory. But to judge him thus superficially is to judge him unjustly. Go a little deeper, and under his seeming restlessness and shiftiness you will come upon accuracy of thought, uprightness of intention, and, possibly, fixity of aim. But it needs a keen-sighted observer to see into those innermost recesses of human nature where the true man, the man worthy of all respect for the simple reason that he is a man, is to be found.

By their speech and action most men show themselves not only fickle, but strangely weak. Yet, from the point of view of the laws a man is seen to break, a man's weakness is one thing; from the point of view of his own conscience, it may be quite another. The narrow-minded are inexorable judges, for they see no farther than the letter of the law, the broader-minded try to look at a fault through the conscience of him who did it. They reproach him with it, but only as a merciful God looks at it, and always light upon extenuating circumstances to make their judgment more indulgent.

Moreover, there are many ways of studying suffering and of realizing what it is — especially interior suffering, pain of mind or heart. There is much, then, for the kind man's mind to do.

The superficially-minded never notice suffering unless it is made a show of; the man who has "fallen among thieves" must cry out very loud or they will pass by without having so much as seen him. The kindly thinker instinctively probes a wound to the bottom; he realizes how, as a general rule, a sorrow is deeper-seated and more keenly felt than it appears; he gently draws aside the curtain under which shyness or suspicion conceal even agony; he has the sharpest of ears for the cry of pain — let the sufferer be as silent and as sullenly suspicious as he may.

To understand a man is to afford him an immense satisfaction. The moment he is understood he begins to feel comforted. It is just because he longs to be understood that it is such a relief to him to tell his troubles. Once understood, he has a weight off his mind. Our being sympathetically told more about ourselves and our troubles than we knew ourselves, and our hearing the story of our sufferings and misfortunes better put than we ourselves could have put it, somehow or another gives us a positive, if indefinable, pleasure.

Even the most fervent of believers likes to feel that, besides God, there is some being who takes notice of him, who understands him, who cares for him, and who values him for whatever steadiness of good purpose his apparent fickleness conceals, for whatever degree of virtue has survived the weaknesses which his many failures witness against him, for whatever little moral strength he displays when beaten down by misfortunes. Now, that someone should show himself intelligently kind and intelligently sympathetic — a form of goodwill possible only where thought is deep and sure — is just what those who have gone under, whether it be through deplorable stupidity of their own, or through cruel misunderstanding on the part of other people, are longing for.

If "the understanding of the poor" be already in itself an act of kindness, it becomes the more kind from the feeling of pity it stirs up in the heart. To show himself pitiful is the kind man's first impulse, and the more he pities, the more generous and more lasting will his kindness be.

No matter whether we be naturally sensitive to other people's pain or the reverse, we are moved to pity them exactly in proportion to what we understand and realize of their sufferings. A glance may suffice to move us to a momentary feeling of compassion; but we must look deeper and linger longer to be able to say with truth that we *feel* for our brother in his trouble.

To be able, then, to think things out clearly and thoroughly makes a man kinder. The deeper one's insight of mind, the more generous one's impulses of heart.

Again, a man's intellect works with his heart to make him kind, by ridding him of certain vain fears and foolish hesitations, which but too often obsess him and tend to paralyze him in the very best of his work.

A child's fear of darkness and its mysteries vanishes with the light of day, and unwholesome thoughts of others, born for the most part of an unworthy oversensitiveness, die away in the clear light of a healthy mind. Among unhealthy states of feeling towards others, the chief are jealousy and touchiness.

Jealousy is the pain which the worth of others causes to the envious. The heart that suffers from this degrading malady makes itself unhappy over the good qualities and successes of others, and takes offence at everything they do. For the jealous man, his rival or competitor is no longer a brother, but a personal enemy whose most trivial doings are irritating, whose very name gives offence, whose manifest virtues are at the least annoying, whose faults are a source of depraved pleasure, whose every rise in life is a torture, and whose humiliation is the one thing longed for.

Jealousy has been rightly likened to the worm that dieth not, for silently it undermines with cruel tortures the wretched soul it invades, in which every feeling of kindness for others is the first thing it destroys. The jealous heart knows no pity, no generosity, no goodwill to man, and most surely no affection, no love. It is wild with passion, yet dead-cold with selfishness. Sullen looks and cutting words, both naturally and by deliberate choice, are its preferred expression; and it all but refuses to conceal its ill will.

A clear-sighted mind has more power than it is generally credited with to cast out from the heart the devil of jealousy, and to fan into a cheerful blaze the dying flame of kindliness.

When tempted to be jealous — for even the best natures are not exempt from such weakness — a wise man will say to himself: "It is every way a good thing that my brother is highly gifted, that the pains he has taken have developed his powers, that his own striving has kept him virtuous. His success he has justly earned. He is a power for good, and the benefactor of many, whether in soul or in body. I have no reason for anything but to be glad at it all. There are in the world only too few capable and active people. No heart should be so evil as to begrudge the good they do.

"I had best applaud with everybody else. After all, I lose nothing because he has got something. Be it that he is better or cleverer than I. There would be no good in dragging everybody down to my own mediocrity. I can gain more by copying him than by being jealous of him.

"In place of letting myself be paralyzed with envy, the thing to do is to try and catch him up."

However tenacious our jealous antipathy, little by little the force of deliberately sympathetic thoughts will wear it away. By enlarging the heart, man's intellect delivers it from unhealthy obsessions.

For touchiness the mind has likewise a remedy. Ill-regulated feelings are often keenly sensitive to the merest mistakes and to the most trifling errors of forgetfulness. Of this, narrow-mindedness is invariably the cause. Why do you feel annoyed? What was there in what was said to hurt you? Why does a man doing a thing in one way rather than another put you out? No doubt you are sensitive. But your outburst of temper was not quite unpremeditated. You had somehow thought over the matter, and it was when you had concluded that you were offended that you writhed with indignation under the insult. It is when you have reasoned out that people have been wanting in consideration for you that you get into a passion. A little more reflection and you would have remained self-possessed, and behaved kindly and properly. You would have seen that such and such words had not the disagreeable meaning you at first sight were inclined to give to them; that you were mistaken as to the reason of such and such proceedings; that in any case the meanings you so readily put upon things were very doubtful. Nay, had you even a certainty that others were intentionally rude or unjust to you, would you not show greater magnanimity of soul and more strength of character by keeping your temper? There is no sense and no display of strength except in keeping one's head in a storm, and in going about as quietly and as methodically as in a calm.

If the intellect helps the heart, the heart, in its turn, is a wholesome school for the intellect. Father Faber goes so far as to say that "nothing deepens the mind so much as a habit of charity." And on his side Auguste Comte maintains that "no great intellect can be developed unless it have a certain fund of kindness to draw upon."

It is, then, a mistake to look upon kindheartedness as giving no more than a gracious charm to character; it is a real source of intellectual light. For kindness develops in man a new sense which in delicacy is second to none. The blind man perceives by touch what his eyes cannot see; and a thousand things in life which escape the mind, the heart knows by its own intuition. Pascal has put a great truth into the well-known words: "The heart has reasons which the reason cannot understand." Indeed, there are two truths here: The *heart* can know things; and the things the *heart* knows man's *mind* cannot always reach to.

The mind of man develops with the treasures of observation and experience he lays up; the richer his store, the more fruitful his output. But the heart's share in getting together these treasures is immense. When, by becoming kind to others, it has refined its oversensitiveness, the heart quickly acquires a delicacy of perception which all other senses lack: half a word is enough for it; it recognizes what is genuine in feelings, no matter by what cloak disguised; it understands embarrassing situations; it thrills when appealed to by emotions barely outlined, and imperceptible to natures less thoroughly developed: it falls into unconscious harmony with interior states which no word has described or defined to it, but which it learns to know by itself entering into them. There revolves, then, within the heart a whole world of impressions, and the heart can communicate to the intellect elements of knowledge which of itself the intellect was powerless to acquire. Its readiness, too, to act, its perseverance, its thoroughness, are qualities for which the mind is debtor to the heart. Practically in life, good-hearted men often show themselves in the end to have understood things better than the merely clever.

II

HOW A MAN CANNOT BE TRULY KIND UNLESS HE HAS THE WILL TO BE SO

Did it not depend on our own free will to be kind or the reverse, kind acts would be purely instinctive. It is because we will to be kind that kindness is, in the true sense, human, meritorious and deserving of esteem.

It is very true that not all kindnesses are equally deliberate; some people have naturally gentle and sympathetic natures — to be kind they need only to follow their own bent. Other characters, sterner and colder, have almost to force themselves to be kind; they are like the seeds which must be ground in a mill before they yield the oil they contain.

Nevertheless, even the naturally kindhearted, those on whom has fallen "the great good fortune to be born good," should bear in mind that to no act of virtue is it natural to be easily put in practice, and that kindnesses are all the more welcome for being premeditated and carried out under difficulties.

Man's will dominates his very soul, and, like the governor of a citadel, controls every one of his powers of action, checking them when unruly, rousing them when sluggish, guiding them, nor allowing them to run to waste. When, then, a man, as he should do, has made up his mind to be kind to all he has to deal with, he should deliberately — and purely because he wills so to do — encourage every feeling of goodwill to his fellow-men, give no ear at all to harsh thoughts, and train himself to distinguish at a glance between true and false kindness.

The noblest souls have had to struggle with themselves before they could be rid of an instinctive tendency to be harsh and ungracious. St. Francis of

Sales avows that to make himself kind and gentle he had to work long and hard. The sympathetic and catholic charity, which is the characteristic of his sanctity, St. Vincent of Paul confesses cost him a wearisome fight. "I turned to God," he says, "and I besought Him earnestly to change my hard and repelling temper, and to give me in its place a meek and gentle spirit, and by the grace of Our Lord, and with a little attention which I myself gave to keep natural impulses well under, I have at least partially got rid of the surly temper with which I was born."

Unkind feelings come over a man without his wanting them, and when he least expects them, and they are of many sorts. Unexplainable antipathies, baseless jealousies, sudden fits of anger, strange tendencies to an uncalled for and systematic opposition — even something almost equivalent to the hating of certain persons, — they are all of

ON THE WAY TO BECOME KIND

them evil growths of our nature, and, albeit our will has had no part in quickening them to their loathsome life, it is by will and by deliberate effort that they have to be uprooted.

It is not enough that a man be convinced in his mind of the folly and shamefulness of indulging in evil thoughts of this sort; it is his duty studiously to reject them. And he must do this at once, for however transient the pleasure wilfully taken in what is wrong, however momentary its mastership of the soul, it leaves its taint behind it, and the door open for its own return. Just as one is bound to put away all positively uncharitable or unkind thoughts, so must one resist the inclination to repress in oneself the impulse to be kind. This strange and really lamentable tendency, which is overcommon, springs mostly from sheer selfishness. In proportion as a man thinks only of himself to the exclusion of others, he becomes blind to their sorrows and to their claims upon him. He sees only the use he can make of them or the trouble they may cause him. If they serve his turn he makes much of them, if he has nothing to gain by them he turns his back on them.

Again, mere love of money may make a man grudge even the time needed to do an act of kindness, for, to be kind, one as a rule must spend both money and time. But most heartless of all the unkind are they who deliberately grind down the faces of the poor, who squeeze out of the labourer the maximum of work for the minimum of wages, who make a business of trading on the weakness or ignorance of the simple-minded and friendless.

Pride, too — that ambition which insists, at whatever cost of truth and, virtue, on being foremost in everything — not only hinders men from being considerate and kind to others, but often tempts them to be cruelly unjust;

to trample on the rights or the dignity of those beneath them, if only to show themselves masters; and, without thought that all men can suffer, to use their victims as mere stepping-stones to their own advancement.

Sensual natures, in fine, are invariably naturally unkind, for the indulging of the baser passions is sure to close the heart to considerateness and to pity. Thoughtlessly at first, but afterwards from sheer wilful malice, the sensual man sacrifices to his own gratification the honour, tranquillity, interest and happiness of those in his power. Into the soul of a man who would lay waste a quiet home without so much as a regret, kind impulses cannot penetrate. Christian charity only grows where the soil is pure and healthy; and it is also in order to make the soil of the heart purer and healthier that one must practise being kind and careful of the happiness and well-being of others.

Even if one cannot at the outset rid oneself of unkind and suspicious imaginings, one can at least always behave kindly to others, and one is bound to take pains to do so. So long as there is war within us, hard thoughts striving to overmaster Christian charity, we must take special heed to what we say and do. We must keep back the bitter and violent words that are on the tip of our tongue, and even more the seemingly calmly thought out and reluctantly made insinuations of evil that mean the death of souls. We must be watchful not to hurt other people's feelings by our proud and haughty looks, bearing, and way of acting. We must never revenge ourselves on anyone, and never, whether openly or secretly, act unfairly by our fellow-men and -women.

By firm self-repression and self-command, whatever our character, we can cease to be positively and habitually unkind. But more has to be done.

ON THE WAY TO BECOME KIND

We must render ourselves absolutely and self-sacrificingly well-disposed to our fellow-men, and for this we must practise the doing of kind actions. Our resolve to learn to be kind must arouse all the energies of our soul, must stimulate us to act, must make us want to carry things by storm.

Plenty of people are gifted with really generous natures, but are temperamentally cold, reserved, awkward. There is a kind heart deep down within them, and those who can get at it may draw upon it without stint; but superficially they appear unfeeling and impassive, and it takes both time and trouble to find out how full of downright goodwill to all they really are. Now, characters such as these carry with them a very grave duty. They themselves have not culpably hidden the talent God has given them; but it is hidden all the same, and it is for them to set to work within themselves and try to bring it to light for their own and their neighbour's good.

Practically, since pity is the first of kind feelings and the first of kind actions, and since from it comes to the human heart the first impetus for good, let the Christian begin to be kind by coming out of his isolation, by seeking out and offering his services to the suffering, the poor, the sick, those who are in trouble, the forsaken, those who have been humbled or put to shame, the mourners, the victims of misfortune, the despairing, those on the brink of crime.

It is not in unadulterated human nature to remain for long face to face with palpable misery without pitying it. A downright hard and depraved heart may remain unmoved; but a heart which is only, as it were, asleep, will rather be wakened up, and will soon beat with kind feeling, that sweetest of rhythms.

ON THE WAY TO BECOME KIND

When once kindness becomes active it is sure to become generous. If it is slow in getting to work, it is for the will to insist, to spur it on. When we cannot give from enthusiasm, let us at least give from sheer logic. A spontaneous gift, the effect of an impulse, is often the more gracious, but a gift, the giving of which has been carefully pondered and perhaps reluctantly resolved upon, is equally meritorious.

Coolly to calculate the cost of our kindnesses is right enough, but by conviction we must be disinterested to the point of sparing neither wealth, health nor work wheresoever the doing of good to others is obligatory upon us. Our forgetfulness of self is of none the less worth because it is a command laid upon us, and by us simply obeyed.

You who are not naturally kindhearted, try to graft kindness onto your temperament, whatsoever it be. Cure yourself of your rough ways of thinking and of acting; they are only the shell that needs to be broken in order to get at the good heart God has in reality given you.

Encourage that same good heart to betray itself in compassionate looks, in sympathetic composure of feature, in unaffectedness of manner, in evenness of temper, and in kindliness of speech.

Everything about you ought to be pleasing. You ought to receive people affably, and to talk to them about what they want to hear. If you would do better still, try to show those with whom you have to deal that you do not consider this tiresome, that they do not weary you when they pour out long confidences in your ears, and that they must not imagine it would be a happy release for you to be left alone.

When our kindness has come to mean all this, far from being a burden to any, we shall be a sure refuge to many; far from often wounding, as hitherto, by heedless word or deed, we shall everywhere in our measure promote the happiness and the moral well-being of our fellow-men.

Nevertheless, it always remains true that, until we have learned by persevering practice to be truly and wisely kind, we shall often have to do wholesome violence to our very nature to show ourselves kind at all; and whether kindheartedness be natural to us, or whether in us it be wholly an acquired virtue, it will ever want watching to keep it straight.

Such watchfulness has to be specially strict in the case of passionate and impulsive natures, always liable to break the fetters of reason and virtue.

Quick, generous, impetuous natures, ready at one moment to overpower by a kind attentiveness almost bordering on the indiscreet, may at another give way to a sensitiveness which is mere selfishness, and selfishness only half-disguised. Like other virtues, true kindness keeps a happy medium. Later on we shall try to show that foolish good nature and unwise indulgence of others is not kindness, but its counterfeit.

Once more, it is necessary that a man should himself think and will so that he may put order and harmony into his goodwill for others.

III

HOW TRUE KINDLINESS IS A QUALITY OF THE HEART

However true it be that both clearness of intellect and strength of will must contribute to make a man considerate of others and good to them, nevertheless kindliness, to deserve its name, must strike its roots deep down in the heart. His understanding shows a man how and where to be kind; by his will he stimulates or restrains, as needed, the impulse he feels to be kind to his fellow-men; but it is only because he is by nature or by grace *kindhearted* that a man can be truly and perseveringly kind.

We speak of a man's mind as being enlightened, of his will as being strong, but only of his heart as being kind.

Words of comfort, good advice, helpful gifts, unless coming from the heart, move us not at all. This is so true that to say a man has no heart, and to say that he is unkind, is one and the same thing.

When, without thinking, you assert quite naturally that such and such a person is kind-hearted, if you just ask yourself how you know he is kind, and why precisely you call him kind, you will see at once that it is at his sensitiveness to the pain of others, at his generous forgetfulness of self, at his affectionateness of disposition — all qualities of the heart — that you have been looking.

A kind heart is easily moved; every sort of distress touches it; tears it can rarely resist; it is, in a word, wholly sympathetic, wholly pitiful.

On the other hand, kind people are themselves easily pleased; every little show of attentiveness wins them over; they are the firmest of friends, in a word, impressionable beings with feelings so marvellously adjusted as to be sensitive to every least breath, whether of sorrow or of joy. The truly kind heart is quick to act; it is fruitful in good works; it delights in noble thoughts, generous designs, daring inspirations — often, maybe, impossible to actuate, but worthier far of human nature than the carefully calculated projects of the cold-hearted.

Feeling and persuasive words come quite naturally to the kind man; he is convincing, comforting — at times even eloquent. If you want a man to resolve upon following your advice, speak to him kindly.

In his eagerness to do good to others, a truly kind-hearted man will spend and sacrifice himself unsparingly, and will show himself equally fearless in danger and self-effacing where there is question of praise or reward.

The kind-hearted, as we have said before, quickly come to feel positive affection for all those they benefit. Their kind acts are not only unselfish because disinterested, but lack the inevitable coldness of a mere doing of duty.

To be kind, even if the thing to be done be of its nature irksome, comes easy to them; for it is inspired by affection, and their kindness is sure to be welcomed, if only because it bears the stamp of a kind heart.

When you speak of a man of good heart, you rightly mean a kind man, for, as we have now shown, to be good-hearted and to be kind are one and the same thing.

But why, after all, should kindness and generosity be said to have their seat or their root in the heart? Is the heart of flesh which beats within our breast anything more in this respect than a symbol agreed upon to stand for kindness? We know that physically it is the faithful echo of all our emotions. May it not likewise in a certain sense be their organ and their instrument? In any event the material heart is sensitive to a degree. Like the delicate instruments which faithfully register the slightest trembling of the surface of the globe, the heart notes and measures the faintest emotion agitating the human soul.

When a man is astonished his heart beats more slowly; when he is violently startled it may even stop; the hearing of good news accelerates its movement; strong passion makes it throb madly; to no mental impression is it indifferent. If you want to know exactly what a person is feeling, place your hand on his heart: his face will not betray him nearly so surely or so readily. Besides, the heart does not keep its secrets; it passes them on to the rest of the man. Formed to draw into itself and to pump out the blood in which is the life of man, the heart directs the vivifying stream into every single member, and all bodily well-being depends upon the accurate regulation of this supply. From a well-formed heart the vital fluid gushes healthily; through shrivelled heart-valves it merely trickles; according as the heart is strong or weak, its blood output is generous or poor; according as it beats quickly or slowly, the flow is rapid or sluggish....

In our own day has originated among Christians the religious movement urging them to be specially devout to the Heart of their Master. For all of the genuine kindlinesses which have ever brightened the world of others, there are none so deep, none so all-embracing, none that have so touched the hearts of men, as the kindnesses of the Heart of Jesus. Christ on earth was invariably kind to everybody; He died out of sheer kindness to men; to those who seek to be His very own, there is no thought so comforting as the remembrance that He is essentially kind. No wonder that men and women, grateful for the great gifts bestowed upon them by the goodness of Christ, should love to trace these gifts to their source and come adoringly to slake their thirst at the Sacred Heart.

If of kindliness we only possess and can only give out what our own heart contains, our wish to acquire the virtue of kindness must needs make us wish for a feeling heart. Now, can we do anything at all to our own hearts?

Both the material organ termed the heart and the moral tendencies somehow bound up with it are fashioned by the successive action of three distinct forces — birth, education, free will. . . .

ON THE WAY TO BECOME KIND

Just as the cutting we plant, once it has taken root, reproduces as it grows the characteristics of the parent stem, so it is with the human being. From the rosebush we have roses, and from the vine we have grapes; even so, the child sooner or later surely brings forth the fruits the history of its race teaches us to look for. . . .

"For good or for evil," says Joseph de Maistre, "at three years old a child's character is formed." If we like we may say rather that it is completely outlined, though not yet filled in, since education and environment have still to do their work upon it, and since, in fine, every man's personality is in his own power.

However fixed the species of plants, everybody knows that care and skilled culture can modify their qualities and produce them in pleasing variations.

In the same way the child is susceptible to influences brought to bear upon it, and whatever its inheritance of character, it responds energetically to the action of the physical or moral forces to which it is subjected. Climate, food, exercise, build up its organism, interior and exterior; the city-bred child differs from the country-bred; the child who day after day breathes the foul air of a factory seems an inferior being to the little creature who revels from morning to night in the sun-kissed air of the fields.

Nor do moral surroundings tell less on the formation of character. Some homes seem made on purpose to develop selfishness in a child, while in others everything tends to the awakening and encouraging of generous feelings.

Take a child who gets everything it wants, whose whims are studied so that they may be at once gratified, for whom all suffering is vigilantly guarded against, who is allowed to think that the world is made for it alone: almost perforce it becomes exacting to those who wait upon it, passionately violent if one of its whims is resisted. Again, those around it show themselves cold and indifferent to the sufferings of other people; the child hears those whom misfortune has overtaken more blamed than pitied; no one teaches it by example how to pity or to sympathize; no one suggests to it that there are hungry children to be fed, and that it becomes the well-to-do to speak kindly to and to help the poor. In a school such as this the unfortunate child literally *cannot* learn to be kind. It has no chance of so much as practising that goodness of heart which may be innate in it.

On the other hand, a child brought up by parents themselves affectionate and charitable; who at an early age is taught to feel that it is loved, but that gratitude is expected from it in return; who is forced to learn from experience what it is to suffer and to work; who shares privations with its parents; who is taught to visit those poorer than itself, and to pity their hard lot, and to help them with alms at some little cost to itself; who hears those in trouble through their own fault spoken of with compassion instead of with severity; and who by all these means has, almost from its cradle, had kindly thoughts and sentiments of good feeling towards others day after day stirred up in its soul — a child so truly fortunate is bound to develop into a kindly man, owing a tender heart to the surroundings of his earliest years.

In fine, there comes to all a day when conscience is sufficiently developed, and when, feeling that we are answerable for the use we make of our powers, we enter into possession of ourselves. Henceforth we are emancipated, free to do with ourselves what we like, and no longer, like soft wax, or damp clay, to be fashioned at the will of others.

Birth and education have left ineffaceable marks on us; moreover, certain propensities have become difficult to uproot from the heart, into the very substance of which they have grown in the course of the long years during which that heart was not its own master.

Yet, even when thus left to ourselves, our formation is not complete, and it is for us to master evil tendencies however fully formed and firmly established within us.... If we set to work manfully we can both give ourselves a new character and create a new heart in ourselves.

To effect this we must begin by studying ourselves, in order to know our faults and our resources. We must have an ideal befitting us individually to look up to, for the plan of life varies from man to man according to his aptitudes and circumstances. Lastly, we must set bravely to work, and by uninterrupted efforts repress our instincts for evil, and develop our tendencies for good.

If we bear in mind that, as faith and reason tell us, goodwill to our fellowmen is both the most Divine and most human of all virtues, and that it is, moreover, the fairest flower and the most fruitful joy of life, we shall school ourselves to banish all harshness from our thoughts, words or acts; we shall of set purpose be unselfish, and grow accustomed to consider people and things otherwise than merely in their relation to ourselves; our favourite sights and our favourite books will be those which move the heart, inclining it to be indulgent, pitiful, generous and affectionate. Our one pleasure and our constant aim will be to lessen suffering and to increase happiness. Happily, there is no single human heart, however handicapped by birth or evil surroundings, which cannot by dint of persevering acquire kindliness for its second nature.

IV

HOW IT IS RELIGION THAT MAKES US KIND

The heart is like a spring — it only gives out what it has received. No spring produces the water that flows from it; from whatever depth it wells up, it has begun by falling as rain from heaven. Even so, the kindliness which overflows a human heart comes from above, and should the heavenly rains cease to water that heart, its wealth would soon be spent.

In truth, "none is good save God alone," none other is essentially kind; angels and men are good and kind only so far as they partake of the Divine goodness and of the Divine kindness. Thus Father Faber rightly said that "kindness is the occupation of our whole nature by the atmosphere and spirit of heaven. Nature cannot do the work by herself, nor can she do it with ordinary succours."*

"No one is good," remarks another writer; "no one deserves to be loved unless there are either heaven-sent thoughts in his mind or heaven-directed affections in his will."

God in the beginning endowed man with kindliness of heart. In creating us to His own image He gave to what in us is lofty and good the absolute supremacy over all base and evil instincts. But sin, by overthrowing the order established in man by God, and by drying up the kindly streams which flowed from the Heart of God to the heart of man, brought about the successful mutiny of his less noble inclinations. His animal nature triumphed, or at least boldly asserted itself. Henceforth in every single one

---

*"Spiritual Conferences," chapter II, page 22.

of us there have been two beings, two laws — the one of the flesh, undisciplined, savage; the other of the spirit, reasonable, gentle. The warfare between them is unceasing, and the issue always doubtful. When the flesh gets the upper hand, we cease to feel for our fellow-creatures, we sacrifice anything and everything to the gratifying of our own appetites, we quickly become utterly selfish, imperious, exacting, jealous, vindictive. When the spirit prevails, we cannot but be compassionate, generous, grateful, humble, affectionate, obliging, faithful. His will enfeebled by sin, man could rarely count upon assuring the victory of his better nature. And, as a matter of fact, evil desires let loose soon gained the mastery in the majority of souls. Mankind became cruel, and the peoples of the world sank into heartless barbarism.

But God, in His mercy, had pity on His creatures thus enslaved to their own evil instincts. He resolved to set up anew in the human heart His kingdom of kindness. To work at this, as it were, with His own hands, God made Himself man like unto us. The Incarnation and the Redemption are in two senses mysteries of kindness, for they are the visible expression of the All-Kind Heart, and they tend essentially to fill anew with goodwill the heart of man. Christ coming among us brought back to this earth the kindness of thought, word and action which long since had vanished from it.

He began by showing how kindness was literally incarnate in His own Person. In His perfectly balanced nature the spirit ruled over the flesh absolutely, and the flesh uncomplainingly obeyed. He set up in the world the one great example of unvarying nobleness of thought, of imperturbable presence of mind, of supreme tranquillity of soul. Further, by persistent example, he taught pity for the suffering, mercy for sinners, tender love of the poor, patience under persecution, silence when outraged, until His love of men made Him lay down His very life to save them. No words can describe Him so truly as His own: "I am the Good Shepherd." His dying on the cross was a free act of compassionate and generous goodness to men. Among His last words were the kindest, the most considerate ever uttered by the lips of man: "Forgive them, for they know not what they do." His teaching He summed up in what we may call His sermon on goodwill to men. "This," He said, "is My commandment, that you love one another, ... for by this shall all men know that you are My disciples if you have love one for the other."

A kindly and affectionate manner is therefore the distinguishing mark of a Christian. He who does not love his neighbour, even though he be always praying, is not a Christian! He only who is good and kind to all is truly Christ's, for Christ has made him what he is.

Imbued with this doctrine, His disciples went forth to conquer the world to charity. They wanted nothing in return. They did not say to their converts, "You shall be our subjects; and we will together set up a great empire, and together will in the end possess the whole earth."

Their message was: "Up to now you have been the slaves of your own flesh, you have served in shame, and in your turn have been cruelly hard to your fellow-creatures; but now that kindliness has once more sprung up on earth in the human nature of Jesus Christ our Saviour, shake off your chains, free yourselves, respect your own selves, and be good to all others. The Master's whole law comes to this, 'that you love one another.' Do so as you should; and no more will be asked from you."

ON THE WAY TO BECOME KIND

So spoke in their day the first messengers of Christ. Their words penetrated the hearts of all who heard them, and forgetfulness of self in the interest of others became the ruling passion of the early Christians. Not only were fervent prayers for the growth of mutual love among them put up day by day, but each morning a table was spread before them that they might each one of them feast on a Food Itself the Incarnate Love of God. The Eucharist is at once the symbol and the source of all goodwill to men, and they who eat of It make their very own the charity of Christ Himself. Hence it has come about that where these heavenly influences have had scope for their play, human nature has grown refined and sympathetic; and men and women have learned to treat one another like brethren, instead of hating one another like enemies. The transformation of mankind has indeed been slow, and is assuredly still far from complete; nevertheless, it is real and palpable enough amongst Christian nations.

The more a nation comes under the influence of Christ, the more striking and universal the spirit of kindliness which pervades it; the greater everyone's respect for the lives and interests of others, the more general are gentleness and courtesy of manner, and the more elaborate and extensive the machinery for the relief of distress.

On the contrary, a people that either has remained a stranger to Christ, or has thrown off His sweet yoke, is sure to be a prey to savagery, either in its old and repulsively brutal form, or disguised as a heartless refinement of modern civilization.

God, who in the beginning implanted goodwill to his fellows in the heart of man, and who by means of the Christian religion has willed to restore its kindly reign upon earth, must ever be the one inexhaustible principle of all kindliness of heart; and to Him, he who wants to learn to be kind must have recourse.

In the Catholic Church, the Heart of Christ is the ever-flowing fountain of all goodness, and gives of its treasures of kindliness to all who reverently and trustfully come to it to slake their thirst.

People are to be met with who, whilst giving themselves to the practices of religion, offend seriously against kindness, either by unworthy thoughts of others, or by indiscreet talk, or by harsh action. But the lives of such persons are in plain contradiction to their pious professions; either they have acquired not more than the outermost shell of piety, and aim at nothing more real, or, however sincere their piety so far as it goes, it is not strong enough to silence the noisy pretensions of a still half-untrained nature.

On the other hand, it is not to be denied that some men, dead to religion, give frequent practical proofs of kindheartedness. For some souls are of their very nature gentle and disposed to oblige; and there are others who, all unconsciously, have retained an imprint of Christian charity so deep that it must not surprise us if instances of perfect kindliness of heart be from time to time met with in what seem utterly heathen surroundings.

Nevertheless, these are only welcome exceptions, and by no means the rule; for the fact remains that religion is the only power in the world really efficacious for the subjugating of unkindly natures; and that for a determined soul a frankly religious life will, by the graces which it calls down from heaven and by the efforts of the will which it imposes, always be the only proper means for the acquiring of the virtues of gentleness, compassionateness, generosity and self-sacrifice.

ON THE WAY TO BECOME KIND

Montalembert, in his "Monks of the West," has ably set forth this aptitude of religion for making men kind to one another: "The happiness of belonging to God," he says, "in no way shuts up a noble heart against the sufferings of others, nor hinders it from sharing any generous emotion.... On the contrary, such a heart becomes more tender and more intimately sympathetic with the hearts of the sorrowful in proportion as it entwines itself more passionately round the Heart of Jesus.... Any spirituality which renders the soul hard, arrogant and devoid of pity is essentially false, as is every religion which dries up or hardens the hearts of its followers...."

Indeed, in taking possession of a soul, piety imprints its distinctive seal of goodwill to men on every single faculty. The lessons which it teaches, the graces which it communicates, the duties which it imposes, combine to make kindliness the dominating characteristic of the Christian life.

The pious soul is in an especial manner learning its lesson in its Master's school in time of prayer and of spiritual reading. And of all the words of Jesus, it loves best to repeat those insisting on gentleness and kindness: "Learn of Me, for I am meek and humble of heart.... I send you as lambs amongst wolves.... Blessed are the peacemakers, for they shall be called the children of God.... Blessed are the merciful, for they shall obtain mercy.... In your patience you shall possess your souls." The Catholic Church is always repeating her Divine Founder's words, and needs must that a docile mind, fed on like maxims, sooner or later will conceive a dislike for any sort of hardness, and will set its true value upon kindness.

To the lessons He vouchsafes to give, God adds the grace of His own visits to hearts that are kind. For He makes Himself present to all who invoke Him. The Prophets even of the old law proclaimed, "Neither is there any other nation so great, that hath gods so nigh them, as our God is present to all our petitions" (Deut. iv. 7).

The intimate intercourse between God and him that prays is much more clearly affirmed in the Gospel: "For where there are two or three gathered together in My name," said Our Lord, "there am I in the midst of them." "If anyone love Me, he will keep My word, and My Father will love him, and We will come to him, and make Our abode with him."

The union of the Christian with his God is still more sensible in Holy Communion, since therein the living Body of Christ, filled with the treasures of the Divinity, becomes the food of man.... And interpenetrated in its inmost being by Divine Love, as metal melts in a furnace, the hardest of human hearts softens and emerges meek and gracious to all.

Again, as hard and barren lands are in time softened and made fruitful by a moist and genial climate, so do the streams of grace infallibly soften the human heart, and make to germinate the seeds of kindliness buried in it.

Or, as a wild beast which has found its tamer unresistingly suffers itself to be mastered, so our nature, when subdued by God, silently submits and puts itself wholly in His hands.

The result of the coming of God into a soul is the re-establishment of order among its powers, the vindication of the right of the mind to rule over the passions, the giving of the upper hand to kindness in our judgments of others and in our way of acting towards them. Nay, since in giving us Christ Himself for our food our religion makes us "eat of goodness, meekness, mercy and love," our whole moral temperament must of necessity be changed for the better.

Lastly, religion imposes tasks in return for the heavenly gifts it bestows; it asks for acts implying moral effort. Nor is it other than just that, after admitting us to a Divinely spread board, it should require something from us. Now the acts of virtue in relation to our fellow-men which religion asks the practice of from us are chiefly, that we quench in our hearts the fires of hatred and jealousy, that we forgive injuries, that we refrain from cutting words, that we be kind to others, and that we endeavour, even at the cost of time and trouble, to succour them in their needs. Note how in making of these things duties for us religion is simply bidding us to be kind and good one to the other.

Religion and kindness go, therefore, hand-in-hand. So great, indeed, is this mutual dependence that there can be no true kindness without God, neither can God be where kindness is not.

You, then, who want to be kind of heart, go and by prayer draw kindness from its source, which is the Heart of God. You, again, who try to be kind and good to your fellow-men and yet fancy that God is far from you, search more deeply into your own soul; God is surely there, hidden though He be, and the day will come when you will reach Him. You, lastly, who flatter yourself that you possess God, and yet are pitiless, unkind, harsh, I say to you that your so-called religiousness is an illusion, for as long as kindness is not in you, God is not with you. The fundamental principle of Christianity and the unmistakable mark of a religious-minded man is his charity to all.

Chapter IV

ON THE COUNTERFEITS OF KINDNESS

I

WEAKNESS OF CHARACTER

"OF ALL difficult things," says Jules Simon, "the hardest is to know where kindness ends and where weakness begins." At first sight weakness mostly looks just like kindness. It is careful not to give pain where it touches, and we are so accustomed to finding thorns strewn on our path that we are grateful to it accordingly. It keeps open house, and a table of which all may share; everyone goes in and out freely. It puts everybody at his ease, it bears with everything, and stands in nobody's way. Just because it never opposes, it makes no one suffer, and so passes for kindness. Yet in reality weakness and kindness are widely different things. Weakness is cold and emasculated; kindness is gentle but strong. The former is essentially characterless; the latter has features pleasingly rounded indeed, but none the less sharply defined. The qualities of the one are all negative, those of the other are positive, and, moreover, stand out in high relief.

Weakness is inactive; it produces nothing, it likes best to gaze placidly at other people working. Weakness is easily preyed upon indeed, but one cannot properly say that a weak man is unselfish. If he is so far moved as to be really sorry for someone's suffering, his pity invariably stops short of making any serious effort to give relief; the knowledge that a fellow-man is in the direst need will not make him really generous, much less venturesome, though he may be not ill content that his goods are of service to others and even that he is forced into doing something. His emotions, though genuine enough, are irremediably slack; self-sacrifice is utterly beyond him.

Kindness, on the contrary, is an active virtue; it is only calm outwardly because all the inner emotions of the truly kind man are well under control; it springs from quiet, well-regulated strength, and can always when needed rise to sacrifices. Whether it merely move to pity, or push to an heroic immolation of self, or be the root of affection and devotedness, kindliness is ever a characteristic of an intense life — calm, indeed, but keen and strong.

The rule of a weak man is marked by lack of restraint, by want of discipline, by disorder, and invariably in the end by general discontent. Everyone suffers where government is weak, because all mistrust where all feel that there is no firm hand on the reins. A rule that is kind means regularity insisted upon, but without harshness; love of discipline and order and peace. Where virile strength is tempered by kindness, all feel the touch of the governing hand, but it does not cramp much less crush them. Obedience and respect are gladly rendered to a kind ruler, and people are happy under him.

In dealing with human beings weakness and kindness proceed on radically divergent lines, and reach diametrically opposite results.

Weakness does not insist upon exertion, and by consequence favours idleness, emasculates the faculties, tolerates improvidence, and unfits one for the battle of life. The mother who spares her child all wholesome suffering, privation, sacrifice, gratifying its every wish and giving in to all its whims, is weak, not kind. She is preparing her child for an impossible bed of roses, and not for the toilsome workshop of life. The teacher who dictates question and answer alike to his pupil, sparing the latter all the work of looking up ref-

THE COUNTERFEITS OF KINDNESS

erences and of expressing in his own words what he learns, is weak and not kind. His exercise-books may be faultlessly filled, but the pupil's mind remains without culture and without tone.

The good-natured but careless giver of alms who pours all the money he is asked for into the hands of the poor, even though thereby he demoralize them by keeping them from looking for work which he had better have helped them to find, is not kind, but weak. For it can never be too strongly insisted upon that we do a grievous wrong to our neighbour, and are anything but really helpful to him, if we lower him by making him the recipient of a seeming charity which is only our own good-natured weakness plausibly disguised.

The kindness which is born of a generous but enlightened will acts on totally different principles. It purposes, before all else, to insure in every way the true good of those on whom it heaps its favours. Assuredly it aims at making people happier, but it also wants to make them braver, more energetic, more self-reliant, and more anxious to develop their own powers. It refuses no wholesome comfort, no healthy stimulus; it praises, it encourages, it cheers, it gives pecuniary help where necessary, but it refrains jealously from doing aught that might give momentary relief at the cost of paralyzing natural activities and enervating the powers of the soul. Far from enfeebling its recipients, such kindness urges them on, dilates their hearts, and perfects them as rational beings.

A father is really kind when, by dint of love and sacrifices, he makes of his child a lover of work, and brings out in him the promise of an energetic personality. A teacher is really kind when, by persevering care, and in due course by unbending insistency, he develops his pupil's initiative. A benefactor best deserves the name when he puts the poor people who appeal to him in the way of using their own strength to earn their own living.

Kindness of the sort we have described — and it is the only sort that is genuine — presupposes true elevation of soul; petty minds as a rule are simply good-natured. It is, therefore, important that, since feelings which have their seat in the heart are of their nature blind and inconstant, one should not wholly trust them, but rather construct in one's mind an ideal of kindness, and with all the strength of one's will determine to be kind in that way and in no other.

The naturally kind-hearted man, who, nevertheless, has no proper idea of what kindness is, mostly goes quite astray, squanders his money uselessly, and does more harm than good. Again, however well-intentioned, however easily moved to pity, the man who can never say

"No," or who has not made up his mind to think before he gives, will find in the end that no one is grateful to him, for the very reason that in reality he has benefited no one.

On the other hand, we must be on our guard lest, under the pretext of not showing ourselves weak, we speak or act harshly. Though the best form of kindness be that which braces its recipient, let us beware lest our hand fall so heavily on the bruised reed we grasp as to snap it.

The deliberateness with which it is done is not the first charm of a kindness, let it be ever so much hidden by the gentleness, patience and unselfishness which hallow it.

In old people, however, kindness goes well with a certain show of weakness. We expect a grandmother to be even more yielding than a mother. Tenderness alone becomes old people's kindness. And it is almost the same with the priest, who is the minister of

THE COUNTERFEITS OF KINDNESS

forgiveness. In the service he renders to God's people, benignity should overrule strength of mind, or rather, strength of mind should express itself in terms of persistent mercy and devotedness. In regard to the faults of his flock, a priest has to show himself neither rigid as an officer to his men, nor exacting as the master of a factory to his hands.

Without changing its nature, kindness should know how to take the various forms suited to differences of persons and of circumstances. Nothing is more opposed to true kindness than that brusque manner of acting which so often masks real weakness of character, since it is of the very nature of interior strength to be unvaryingly self-possessed. The truly kind man is resolute and wise in his thought for others; he is therefore at all places and times gracious and obliging.

II

FLATTERY

Flattery, like weakness, is but counterfeit kindness, though sometimes hard to detect and set aside as such.

The flatterer is affable and courteous like the kind man, but while the address of the latter has a charm and a nobleness all its own, the flatterer is instinctively distrusted and despised. The one and the other praise, but if the praise of the man who truly loves and respects you is like a refreshing cordial, that of the flatterer is an intoxicating and often poisonous drug.

"Few men," says Father Faber, "can do without praise." Scrupulous souls, unhappy over their involuntary shortcomings, and alarmed about their smallest faults, would lose heart and let themselves be utterly crushed under the weight of their own foolishness, if from time to time they were not braced

THE COUNTERFEITS OF KINDNESS

up by a little wholesome praise, and encouraged to trust God and persevere. Timid, hesitating souls would shrink unduly from publicity, and precious powers for good would remain undeveloped and unused, if opportune praise did not wake up self-assurance in them, and set their wealth of energy to work.

All who are worn out with toil, disheartened by criticism, put out of countenance by systematic contradiction, worried by the temptation to give up undertaking anything in order to sink into unnoticed torpor, are in downright and possibly urgent need of a kind and compassionate friend who, holding out a helping hand to them, will by consoling words rally their hope and strength, and drive home the conviction that for them life is not yet exhausted, and that it still depends on themselves whether they give up for good or play manfully as they should their part in the world....

But nothing needs more delicate handling than praise. It is one of the functions of kindness so to mete it out that it may stimulate without intoxicating. Administered carefully and in moderation, above all with sincerity, it may well be the herald of happiness and a spur to virtue. But unmerited and unwise praise is not kindness; it has degenerated into flattery.

The flatterer always exaggerates; if it is real merit on which he dilates, he either goes glaringly beyond what he should, or tactlessly repeats over and over again one and the same compliment: if there is really nothing to praise, he will extol weakness itself, and not content with finding excuses for faults, rather than fail in praising, make virtues out of vices, nor stop till both truth and fancy are exhausted.

Some people flatter from sheer thoughtlessness and because they have learned no better. They only want to please, and the outcome mostly is that they are not believed, and finish by looking foolish and undignified.

But there are times when flattery is inspired by cold calculation and truly contemptible self-seeking; it is then above all that it is base and culpable. To gain a man's favour, to insure his support, to get hold of his money, flatterers flock round and fawn on him, deceive him, and turn his head with lying praises.

The flatterer's feelings have nothing to do with such adulation, it is literally only lip praise. Unstable as it is insincere, it gives place to venomous criticism the moment its object ceases to be of use and some fresh interest comes into view. He who has fallen thus far is a parasite, a man of essentially mean and contemptible soul.

However given, flattery is always prejudicial to its recipient. It may be but unsubstantial smoke, but it intoxicates and is breathed in gratefully, and even greedily. The majority of men are so taken by it that they cannot discern between the restrained praise given in wise kindness and the flattery born of thoughtlessness, irony or self-seeking.

Even the cleverest people at times allow themselves to be deceived by flattery. However clear-sighted any of us may be in other matters, we are purblind to flattery; when people who have something to gain by pleasing us, bait their trap with honeyed words, the wisest of us may fall into it. Besides, we really like to be deceived about ourselves; we are only too glad to forget our own failings, to ignore the narrow limits of our abilities, to have our own worth proved to us, and to hear that even our everyday life is worthy of note!

The great mischief of it all is that we become overconfident of ourselves, and that, overstepping the boundary line of our abilities, we rashly engage in adventures beyond us, to end not only in failure but in getting ourselves laughed at.

Flattery deceives all the more easily because it brings on a sort of intoxication. Or, more truly, it is like those poisonous drugs which for a little while seem to warm the very heart, and impart a delusive strength, only to end by chilling a man's lifeblood, lowering his vitality, and depressing or rather prostrating his whole being. The reaction from the fleeting buoyancy of spirits due to our acceptance of flattery is often the more bitter because commonly he who has flattered us is the first to betray us, and, if he can gain thereby, to turn our best friends against us. The ancient aphorism is true: "A man has no worse enemies than they who flatter him."

Seeing, then, to what evils inconsiderate praise may lead, let us always be affable and well-spoken, but never flatter. Our praise should be a wholesome encouragement, not a poison.

III

INDISCREETNESS

Kindness, even when indiscreet, is very different from flattery; in itself it is neither mean nor prejudicial. Nevertheless, to have been performed indiscreetly takes from both the worth and the delicate charm of an act of kindness. To be discreetly kind is to be doubly kind, for the value of a gift is halved if the manner of giving make it a burden.

Benefactors, however lavish in their gifts, have barely a right to the name if they load their benefactions with irksome conditions. Others, again, there are who multiply their benefactions beyond all requirement; not satisfied with helping, they overpower: they not merely relieve the poor, they tire them out with their visits. Thinking to be kind, they make themselves a nuisance. They treat their protégés as if they were so many children. Their permission or, as they call it, advice, has to be asked about everything. In return for what they give they expect not only gratitude and deference but absolute submissiveness. Their hand is heavy. They allow no initiative. Firmly convinced that by settling beforehand all important questions regarding those they befriend they further the interests of the latter, they prevent them from living their own lives, and, so far as they can, turn them into mere machines.

A man is kind in his almsgiving in proportion as he makes the poor man he relieves feel that what he receives becomes his very own. On the contrary, he is fundamentally unkind if he paralyzes instead of stimulating by what he gives and by his way of giving.

We avoid being the first to put out our hand in welcome to the man who, to demonstrate the exceptional warmth of his friendship, crushes the hand he grips in place of shaking it; his intention is all that it should be, his disinterestedness is beyond question, but he needs to be enlightened as to the fitting way of expressing the kindliness of his feelings.

From the dealings with man of God Himself, one can easily gather that the aim of all kindness is to make life fuller, and that true kindness respects the individual, makes the best even of his oddities, and furthers the development of all that is of value in his character.

How discreet after its fashion is a humble wayside spring! Its freshness invites the traveller to slake his thirst. It gives him all it possesses, he may even provision himself from it for the longest of journeys. If it were endowed with understanding, what satisfaction would it not feel at having refreshed a man, and restored his strength, and at seeing that, thanks to the virtue of its waters, he is able joyfully to continue on his way! It asks nothing at all in return; what it did for one man yesterday it will gladly do tomorrow for another, always pleased to give, always satisfied with the privilege of helping.

As not less discreet we may picture the vivifying air we take into our lungs. We are surrounded by it, immersed in it. It penetrates us, it responds to the needs of our organs; far from weighing us down, it supports us. Invisible to our eyes, it shuts nothing out from our sight. It makes us live; it never stands in the way of our living to the full.

Water and air are but symbols. In God Himself we have an example of a kindness infinitely discreet. God is pre-eminently our Benefactor. He has given us life; we hold all our faculties from Him; at each moment He confirms to us the gift of existence; His graces are continuously poured upon us; only with His help can we do any good at all. And yet, all this notwithstanding, He respects us absolutely; though ever accessible to those who seek Him, yet He never imposes His presence on any man's conscience. He solicits us unceasingly, but He never forces our will; no life could develop without Him, and yet He leaves to each one of us freedom to live up to whatever standard we please. Truly God shows us what we have to do to work wisely upon others. His kindness is watchful, long-enduring, all-embracing; so should ours be. His kindness is never wearisome, never interfering, never burdensome; neither should ours be.

IV

EMOTIONAL AFFECTION

There is one more sort of counterfeit kindness leading to mistakes both very common and very dangerous. We think we are sacrificing ourselves, whilst in reality we are seeking self-gratification; we flatter ourselves that we are acting out of pure love of our neighbour, whereas, as a matter of fact, we are merely aiming at our own satisfaction. It is not that our heart is touched, it is only that our nerves are excited; our self-love is masquerading as Christian charity. We think ourselves good and kind, but alas! we are only selfish. What we want is to feel good, and to enjoy feeling so.

It is not that nobility of feeling is incompatible with earthly affection. By no means, since earthly affections are lawful and even God-commanded; but certain natures have to be specially on their guard, for a feeling of particular sympathy may be with them a mere cloak under which passion shelters itself, in order both to deceive the would-be kind man himself, and to throw dust in the eyes of others.

Kind feelings deepen the heart, and open it to the realizing of every sort of suffering. "The heart is enlarged," says Joubert, "by the very fact of its love and pity being for many." By becoming universal one's kindheartedness suffers no decrease, so far as regards any one of its objects, for the power it has of loving all mankind takes nothing from its intensity of affection for any one of our neighbours in particular.

Emotional affection, on the contrary, confines the heart within the narrow circle of some "special friendship." Obsessed by one object, it is unable to stretch farther its love, and not only is its kindliness limited to one object, but it opposes a hard, repellent exterior to everything besides, however worthy of a share of its affection.

The spirit of goodwill to men is the health of the soul, and dwells within it in calm peace and joy; it is moved to pity, but is never ruffled; it works hard, but is never restless; its absolute disinterestedness saves it from feeling the bitterness of the many deceptions it suffers.

True kindness makes no distinction of age or sex; it sees only that others are in need, and, touched by their distress, gives to all alike generous and gracious aid; it inhabits a region far above the realm of the senses.

Emotional affection, on the contrary, is the principal factor in what spiritual writers term "particular friendships," in which not the heart but the senses are moved, and moved by what appeals to them rather than to the higher powers of the soul. Such affections are quite other from Christian kindness, and are of their nature perilous from the circumstance that, being more in the flesh than in the soul, they are less under the empire of the will.

Sentiments of Christian affection are born but slowly, and are easily traced to their origin, which is invariably either well-grounded pity or well-merited esteem. The birth of a purely earthly attachment, on the other hand, is as sudden as it is inexplicable. Lacordaire has aptly said: "The heart is like a thunderbolt; we never know where it will fall until it has fallen."

Now we do know what the things are which go to make men kindhearted — a busy and a serious lifework, the habitual mastering of our feelings, the practice of religion. The soul that is healthy, well-ordered and pious is sure to be kind.

"Idleness hath taught much evil," says Holy Writ. The soul that is unoccupied is like a field that is lying fallow and unfenced; weeds and brambles spring up and overrun it of themselves, and destructive beasts prowl about it.

If sensual love is the ruin of those who give themselves up to it, Christian kindness is the true preservative of the soul. It makes happy both the giver and the receiver; it is good alike for

THE COUNTERFEITS OF KINDNESS

man's mind, for his heart, for his will, for his dignity, and for his virtue.

Kindness, then, bids us hold our heart in our hands, and at the same time wisdom bids us keep a hand on our heart. We must be watchful and careful, lest under the guise of kindliness we give the hospitality of our hearts to the most degrading of its counterfeits.

CONCLUSION

TO THE kind reader whom these pages may have interested we have but one word more to say. Open wide your soul to kindliness, and let it enter deeply into your very being.

Do not fear to be kind: to be kind can do you no harm, can bring you no bitterness, nor will you ever repent of it. You will regret having been harsh or weak, but you can never regret having been good to others. If, at times, people mistake your motives, if your kindnesses are forgotten, or repaid with ingratitude, you will nevertheless enjoy the supreme consolation of knowing that you have not sinned against your neighbour.

Love kindliness as the very source of all peace and of all joy. Nothing is so sweet to the mind as a kind thought; nothing rests the will like having rendered a service; nothing

CONCLUSION

touches the heart like one's own feeling of pity; nothing nourishes the soul like noble and devoted affection. You will always feel happier and better for having done a kind action.

Have great faith in the power of kindness; it alone has the gift of captivating hearts. People passionately resist coercion; they obstinately argue with science; but they yield gladly to kindness. If you want to be an apostle, remember that kindliness alone will enable you to conquer souls. Christ, the King of Peace, willed to discover to men only the meekness and humility of His Heart, and He accepts for His apostles only those who are ready to be as "lambs amongst wolves."

If you are convinced of the truth of what you have read in this little book about kindness, make a firm resolution henceforth never to pour one single drop of gall into anyone's cup, no matter whose it may be, and never to suffer a single day to pass without your having shed a ray of happiness on some poor, troubled heart.

www.ingramcontent.com/pod-product-compliance
Lightning Source LLC
Chambersburg PA
CBHW022114040426
42450CB00006B/702